FRANCISCANS UNDER FIRE

*Twenty Nuns,
A Girl
and a Dog*

Also by Duane Hutchinson

Doc Graham, Sandhills Doctor, 1970

Images of Mary, 1971

Exon, Biography of a Governor, 1973

Savidge Brothers, Sandhills Aviators, 1982

Storytelling Tips, 1985

A Storyteller's Ghost Stories, 1987

A Storyteller's Hometown, 1989

Grotto Father, Artist-Priest of the West Bend Grotto, 1989

FRANCISCANS UNDER FIRE

*Twenty Nuns,
A Girl
and a Dog*

The Story of the Sisters of Saint Francis of the Immaculate Conception of the Blessed Virgin Mary, Mount St. Clare, Clinton, IA 1864-1907

from the unfinished manuscript of
Msgr. Mathias Martin Hoffman
as told by
Sister Augusta Carrico, OSF

edited by
Duane Hutchinson

Foundation Books
Lincoln, Nebraska

FRANCISCANS UNDER FIRE: TWENTY NUNS, A GIRL AND A DOG. Copyright © 1990 by Foundation Books, Inc. All rights reserved. Printed in the United States of America. No part of this book may be used or reproduced in any manner whatsoever without written permission except in the case of brief quotations embodied in critical articles and reviews. For information address Foundation Books, Inc., P.O. Box 29229, Lincoln, NE 68529.

Cover design by James W. Hutchinson.

Library of Congress Cataloging-in-Publication Data

Hoffman, M. M. (Mathias Martin), 1889-
    Franciscans under fire : twenty nuns, a girl and a dog : the story of the Sisters of Saint Francis of the Immaculate Conception of the Blessed Virgin Mary, Mount St. Clare, Clinton, IA / edited by Duane Hutchinson ; from the unfinished manuscript of Mathias Martin Hoffman as told by Augusta Carrico.
       p.   cm.
    ISBN 0-934988-21-8 "pbk. : alk. paper"
    1. Sisters of Saint Francis of the Immaculate Conception of the Blessed Virgin Mary (Clinton, Iowa) -- History. I. Hutchinson, Duane. II. Carrico, Augusta. III. Title.
BX4486.76.H64 1990
271'.973077767--dc20

                                                  89-36681
                                                       CIP

FIRST EDITION

Most recent printing indicated by the first digit below:
1   2   3   4   5   6   7   8   9   10

The paper used in this publication meets the minimum requirements of American National Standard for Information Sciences - Permanence of Paper for Printed Library Materials, ANSI Z39.48-1984. ∞

To Sister Augusta Carrico,
who listened and remembered
and to the students
at Mount Saint Clare,
that they may know the story

*The nobleness
that lovely spirits gather from distress.*
— John Masefield

Contents

Foreword _____ xi

Introduction _____ xv

Editorial Method _____ xix

PART ONE
Kentucky

1. Aunt Caroline _____ 3
2. Starting the Order _____ 7
3. Warning of Trouble _____ 11
4. Franciscan Training and a New Home __ 15
5. Caroline Goes to Court _____ 19
6. Write the Bishop Yourself _____ 25
7. A New Home and an Old Rescuer _____ 31
8. To Move or Not to Move _____ 33
9. The Next Casualty _____ 37
10. Controversy Carried to Rome _____ 43
11. Peace and a Word from Papa _____ 49
12. The Death of the Trappestine Dream _ 55
13. Bishop McCloskey Gets His Way _____ 59
14. Like a Thief in the Night _____ 63
15. Fire _____ 67
16. Mother Angela _____ 73
17. Mother Teresa's Crisis _____ 77
18. The Chicago Hill Schism _____ 81
19. The Affair of Father Hugh Daly ____ 87
20. Christian Tact _____ 93
21. Begging _____ 99
22. Brides of Christ _____ 105
23. Yearning for Olivet _____ 107
24. Back to Olivet? _____ 109
25. The Finger of God _____ 117
26. Owls at Olivet _____ 121

PART TWO
Iowa

27.	A Welcome and a Challenge	125
28.	Anamosa	131
29.	The Duel	135
30.	Archbishop Forces Election	139
31.	Interrupted Election	145
32.	A Sad Lesson	149
33.	I Pray for Her Every Day	153
34.	I Want to Go to My Room	157
	Select Time Line	163
	Notes	169
	Appendix. "The Jubilee of an Old Sister"	177
	Index of Names	179

Foreword

When I came to Clinton in 1983 as a storyteller-in-residence with the Iowa Arts Council, I stayed at Mount Saint Clare's Durham Hall. One evening in the college library I asked for a history of the college and of the Order. The student librarian said she thought something was in the archives, but it would take special permission to see.

I asked my friend, Sister Augusta, by now my occasional voice teacher, if she had heard about such an effort. She blushed. "Several criticized the manuscript," she said, "so it was put away. It won't be easy to see." Such a tantalizing remark!

When she handed me her only copy, and a poor fourth carbon at that, her hand actually trembled. "Be careful," she said, "and bring it back in the morning."

That night I read the "forbidden manuscript" as nervously as a teenage boy reading a naughty book. But I soon discovered it was a beautiful story. I fell in love with Sally Walker who became Sister Frances. Yes, there was anger in it, and triumph, and mistakes and courage. Here I found in the tale by Father Hoffman and his friends a story I wanted to tell--not a detailed history, but a good story.

It is really Mother Regis Cleary's story. As Mother Superior of the Order, she asked Monsignor Mathias Martin Hoffman[1] to write the history of the Sisters of Saint Francis of the Immaculate Conception and she oversaw much of his early writing of it.

Monsignor Hoffman was an obvious choice. As rector of Saint Francis Church in Dyersville, Iowa, he was nearby and he had written several books, including *The Story of Loras College, Arms and the Monk! The Trappist Saga in Mid-America* and *Young and Fair Is Iowa*. He took a special interest in Mother Regis' request because of his love for her and her community.

This is also Sister Augusta Carrico's story. She remembered the oral history from the founders and took Sister Caroline Gehringer, Superior of Mount Alverno, to search records in Louisville, Kentucky, and elsewhere. They found a treasure-trove of letters and other documents. They found in the letters evidence of raging controversies and personality conflicts. They chuckled over county records in Louisville describing tracts bounded by creeks, cabins, trees and boulders.

Conversations between Monsignor Hoffman and Sister Augusta took place over a period of years in the Thirties and Forties. Part way through Monsignor Hoffman's writing he discovered he had cancer. He raced against death to write of the Order which had given birth to Mount Saint Clare College and many other institutions. Sister Augusta said, "Sometimes we talked until three o'clock in the morning, so urgent was our task."

Monsignor Hoffman saw the humble Sister Frances (Sally Walker) as the one to tell the story. Sister Frances had carried in her heart the burdens of her troubled Aunt Caroline who had founded the Order in Kentucky in 1864 under the blessing of Bishop Lavialle. She herself had been one of the three founding Sisters. She had shared the good times and the bad in Kentucky. She had made the trek from Kentucky to Iowa in 1890. Sister Frances had prayed for the wayward Mother Agnes who vigorously led the community, yet almost destroyed it. Sister Frances had rejoiced in the saintly Mothers Paul of the Cross Carrico and Magdalen Mattingly.

I photocopied that book. In the morning when I returned it to Sister Augusta, I had to tell her what I had done. She put both hands up to her cheeks and looked at me horror stricken. "I must tell our president, Sister Mary Smith, right away," she said.

Later I heard that President Smith had reportedly said, "Good. It's time the story is told."

So, I put most of the 205 pages into my Osborne computer and began editing. I was happy to discover Mother Magdalen Mattingly's relationship to my friend, the late Chaplain Louis Edward Mattingly of Nebraska Wesleyan University. In writing his biography, I had searched his Kentucky home country of Lexington, south of Berea where I once went to school, and Louisville where lived the noble and generous Mr. Ben Mattingly. Also my great-grandfather Silas Harmon had come to Louisville about the time this story begins to sell his hand-coopered barrels filled with apple cider from his Lexington, Indiana, farm.

Foreword

I wish to give thanks to the Center for Dubuque History at Loras College for permission to edit and publish Monsignor M. M. Hoffman's manuscript, "Twenty Nuns, a Girl and a Dog," and special thanks to Mike Gibson for his help in searching for information.

Duane Hutchinson

Introduction

The blue-black engine proudly puffed across the sturdy steel bridge over the Mississippi River and into the new Illinois Central Station in Dubuque. Behind trailed five yellow passenger cars coming from Chicago. Next to the square brick tower of the station with its gingerbread trim, the engine sent a satisfied gasp of white steam on this snowy afternoon in 1890.

Before the conductor could set down his stepping-stool, twenty smiling nuns bounded out of the last two cars. They were fresh from the heart of Kentucky, but clad in the garb of Saint Francis of Assisi. Mostly young, some middle aged, not one of them was as yet fifty years old. They came tripping and laughing along the platform. The last nun carried in her left hand her little canvas satchel. With her right hand she held the collar of her tail-wagging Saint Bernard. Behind the last nun came a young lady with long black curls and a grey traveling suit.[2]

The nun looked at the station and at the people staring with curiosity from its Roman-arched doors. Then she glanced at the sky and across the snowladen landscape.

"So, this," she almost sang, "is Iowa, the promised land!"

"No," said the young lady with her, "Iowa, the land of promise!"

Next to the platform stood a huge bobsled pulled by a four-horse team. The great animals impatiently stamped in the snow. As the superior of the little order, Mother Agnes, briskly led the way to the waiting sled, several men in the gaping crowd raised their hats in reverential greeting. She smiled and bowed in return. One man spoke to a friend loud enough for Mother Agnes to hear. "A brave little group of women, but rather a strange sight, eh?"

"Why?" asked the other gentleman. "What's strange about it?"

After all, Iowans had witnessed the mass arrivals of newcomers into the state--colorful and sometimes uncouth crowds of strangers--immigrants, landseekers and adventurers, many with their wives and children.

"Oh, not so strange in general," answered the first gentleman, "but strange in this particular: These aren't immigrants; these aren't nuns from France or Germany or Ireland, such as we've been receiving in Iowa. This is an order of American ladies." He snapped his fingers. "Just like that! Pulled up their roots from their old Kentucky homes. Came bag and baggage over here to start a new life for their Faith."

"'Tis strange. How do you know about them?"

"Oh, from Con Shea. He told me all about them."

Con Shea, the cathedral sexton, had driven his bobsled over to meet the Kentuckians. He knew this community was a black swan, an Ishmael, hitherto quaintly unconformable to any pattern. Most American sisterhoods had an oft-repeated pattern. A small group of European nuns would arrive with few resources and sometimes little education. The community would get a toe-hold somewhere and begin with whatever work was at hand. They'd scrimp, save and expand. They'd draw new followers. In time they would establish schools, hospitals and orphanages. The immigrant community in fifty years would become a thriving order with dozens of foundations.

Such was not the pattern of the Kentucky sisterhood. This singular group of women--widows, sisters or daughters of Civil War soldiers--North and South, farm girls, society girls--came from the first settlers who ventured into Kentucky. Their ancestors pioneered with Daniel Boone or with the early missioners, Father Badin and Father Nerincks. They were from the section renowned as the "Holy Land" of Kentucky, whose center was the little old cathedral city of Bardstown. They had lived under the very shadows of the Trappist Abbey towers of Gethsemane, in the region of Nazareth, Loretto and Saint Rose which cradled the Sisters of Charity, the Sisters of Loretto and the Dominican friars and their college of Saint Thomas. They had come from the country sanctified by the names of holy centers such as Saint Charles, Lebanon, Holy Cross and Calvary in Kentucky.

Why had they exiled themselves from the fragrantly hallowed land to face the breeze-swept prairies of Iowa--a land they readily admitted they knew nothing about? Because "Sweet are the uses of adversity." If ever a community of nuns was sweetened by adversity it was these humble but happy Franciscans. For years they had run the gauntlet of misfortune.

Introduction

This order had been the bone of contention between diocesan bishops and mitered abbots, a trouble of Archbishop Spalding of Baltimore and the worry of Archbishop Elder of Cincinnati. Ecclesiastical disputes hovered about them and even reached Rome and the Cardinals of the Propaganda. The infant Franciscan order had struggled for its very existence while others played one side against the other, now supporting the bishop, and then appealing to the abbot, a precarious game bordering disaster.

In the entire American history of religious communities perhaps no other underwent such suffering. They had once enjoyed a measure of security in their manorial-type convent at Mount Olivet, near Gethsemane, Kentucky. At that time happy children raced through their halls and came obediently to classroom and chapel. The cloister was filled with eager novices who looked out at the convent gardens and orchards. Former slaves sang as they worked in the neighboring tobacco fields.[3] Serenity had reigned then and the future looked bright. In a few years these same nuns were starving, almost degraded, with mortgaged and impermanent roofs over their heads. They were compelled to go out into the streets of Louisville and Cincinnati and into the countryside of Indiana to beg for their very living from door to door.

Worse than these physical sufferings, outbursts of bitter antagonism came from the laity. Newspapers pilloried them with insinuations. Criticism and cold aloofness from the Kentucky clergy isolated them. This persecution of the spirit galled more acutely than the refusals of the grocer and the shoemaker to do business.

Such were their years in their homeland of Kentucky, and such was to be their first decade in Iowa, including even an interdict of the bishop after this arrival in Dubuque.

Twenty poor but smiling nuns, a girl and their dog! Since then the order's transplanted roots have gone deep into Iowa soil, and its growth and its fruits have been blessed by God.

Now, there are nuns and there are nuns, for it takes all kinds to make the Church. These Kentucky nuns were a special kind.

The Sisters of Saint Francis, whose motherhouse came to be at Mount Saint Clare in Clinton, Iowa, are the nuns who have lived a remarkable story. This story has really only two chapters--the one about Kentucky and the other about Iowa. Here follows the tale of sufferings and scandals and triumphs, told gently and tolerantly by the humblest nun of them all, Sister Frances--formerly Sally Walker.

Sally Walker, the daughter of Hugh Walker, a slave-owning tobacco planter, was one of the founders during the closing days of the Civil War. She survived all of her early contemporaries and this is the story of her community as she wrote it in part as far as her letters and the documents are concerned. This is the story from her viewpoint as she might have set them down in its entirety.

The documents and letters are quoted verbatim; and most of the conversation reflects almost verbatim the records and written annals of the community. The dialogue of this narration renders the historical material as nearly literally exact as is practical and possible in her story.

It should be said of this nun, Sister Frances Walker, that when she died in 1921, her published obituary stated that her life was remarkable for nothing . . ." With this summation the world might agree; but the obituary article continued: her life was remarkable "for nothing--except humility." And that is the sublime stuff that heroes and heroines are made of.

Msgr. M. M. Hoffman

Editorial Method

My purpose in editing this manuscript has been to strip away opinion and let the story be shown through action and pictures. We do it in the classroom by changing passive voice to active voice, eliminating redundancies and clarifying terms. Monsignor Hoffman would have done it, and better, had he lived to complete the task.

Documents and letters are quoted verbatim, though not in all cases completely; and most of the conversation reflects almost verbatim the records and written annals of the community. The dialogue of this narration renders the historical material as nearly literally exact as is practical and possible in her story.

Sister Augusta says, "Every fact we have in there is true. We have volumes of letters and other evidence to back up what we've said." But this is still not intended to be a full, complete history. I hope that what we've done here will stimulate the writing of a careful history. What is here is a story told by Sister Frances, "the humblest nun of them all."

PART ONE
Kentucky

1.
Aunt Caroline

I was nineteen in 1864 and Aunt Caroline's favorite niece. Caroline Cambron, my mother's youngest sister, had been quite a belle in Nashville. Now she was Mrs. Warren, a war widow. Since she wanted me, Ma and Pa thought I could come over and live with her as a companion and a helper. I'm afraid that all I did at the time was to read what few books came to hand and stitched at fancy work. Oh, yes, I always led the rosary and the songs in the evening because Aunt Caroline and Miss Lillis insisted.

Aunt Caroline managed the school, disciplined the girls, conducted a class or two and sewed for the monks. Miss Lizzie Lillis taught the school and lived with us in our crowded cottage.

Aunt Caroline took me more and more into her confidence. One day she said, "I'm thinking about becoming a nun." I'd heard strange statements from her, but this was the strangest.

"Don't say anything to Miss Lillis, yet," said Aunt Caroline, "but Father Abbot told me it can be done quietly and with little fuss."

"How can you be a nun?" I asked. "You're a married woman! All the nuns I ever heard of--over at Nazareth, for instance--were never married."

"You mean I *was* a married woman, Sally. And," she added, with a bit of asperity, "if I am a widow, I am a decent and respectable one, I hope."

Caroline had been distressed since her husband died in the Battle of Perryville, in October 1862. General Brag personally informed her of Captain Warren's death. A week later she came from Nashville and searched for her husband's grave. We found his marker right on the Marion County line, not far from our home.

Caroline wouldn't go back to the Warrens, because they were Baptists and because of war conditions. She was deeply religious in a way, but narrow. She constantly prayed for the soul of her husband who had refused to embrace our Faith.

Aunt Caroline went to the Gethsemane Abbey early the next spring to have Masses said for her husband. There she met Abbot Benedict Berger. He was so impressed by her commanding appearance that he asked her to be supervisor of the girls' school. She agreed with alacrity and now in 1864, her second year, she was making a success of the school. She loved this type of life and she admired Abbot Benedict and the monks. But she grew severe and ascetical. The idea of becoming some sort of a Third Order of Franciscan religious[4] strongly appealed to her.

Of course, she couldn't keep the secret much longer from Miss Lillis, and soon the three of us were discussing the matter from every angle. This was Lizzie's first year of teaching at the school, and since she knew no more than I did about its history, we both began to ply Aunt Caroline with questions.

"This school," Aunt Caroline said, "has been conducted here since 1855."

"Is that when the Trappist monks came here?" we asked.

"No, indeed. These Trappists, or Cistercians[5] came to Gethsemane from France in 1848 and had no school. They bought Gethsemane Farm from the Sisters of Loretto, founded by Father Charles Nerincks. Then they had fourteen hundred acres of woodland, cornfields and log cabins. Out of these cabins they built their original log-cabin monastery.

"By the way," Aunt Caroline went on, "Miss Lizzie, didn't you come from the school of the Sisters of Loretto?"

"No, Mrs. Warren, I was educated by the Sisters of Charity over at Nazareth."

"Yes, that's right. I had forgotten."

Then my aunt continued her story. "The first abbot of the monks, Father Eutropius, in 1853 traveled over Kentucky and elsewhere collecting funds for the huge abbey now being finished. He promised the contributors--both Catholics and Protestants--that the abbey would conduct a school for poor boys and girls. In his pamphlet he said the girls' school was 'to be conducted by a lady of suitable age, and of unexceptionable piety, virtue and morals.'"[6]

I couldn't suppress a giggle. "I'm sure, Aunt Caroline," I said, "that when they wrote 'a lady of suitable age, and of unexceptionable piety, virtue and morals' they already had you in mind."

"Why, Sally Walker, don't try to be facetious!" My aunt frowned at me. "All the teachers have been good and self-sacrificing women. I knew some of them. Mrs. Rutherford, the first teacher, started out in the small brick house that Abbot Eutropius built on Calvary Hill near the monastery. Miss Louisa Willet, a convert and a lovely lady, conducted the school until 1860 when Father Benedict was elected Abbot. Then he closed the boys' and girls' schools for awhile."

"Why did he do that?" asked Lizzie.

"Because Abbot Benedict is a high-principled and conscientious monk. He knew the Trappist Order is meant for contemplation and fasting and prayer, not for outside business, 'exterior works,' such as schools. His predecessor's promise violated the spirit of the Order. And what was the poor man to do?"

"Well, what *did* he do?" I asked.

"All the proper things," she answered. "He had the matter put before the headquarters of the Order in France, the 'General Chapter,' they call it, and he obtained a sort of quiet permission.[7] But he said he hopes our schools will be taken over by a Sisters' Order and free the abbey of the problem."

When she said this, my mind leaped to the reason Aunt Caroline was quietly resolving to become a nun! This was the first step toward a Sisters' community to take over the girls' school.

Aunt Caroline's respect and admiration for Abbot Berger amounted to a profound veneration. She saw him as the ideal churchman, a model for her growing asceticism. He was a God-fearing, completely self-disciplined priest. She was aiming for the same as a nun.

Father Abbot--Dom Benedict Berger was his Breton name--was an uncompromising disciplinarian in his abbey, a ruthless defender of the rigor of the Rule. Then, and later on, he impressed me as a kind-hearted monk with a Napoleonic chin and steely eyes. But, I dreaded the thought of a clash between him and Aunt Caroline--both stubbornly ascetic souls--and I was later justified in that dread.

"Our school," said Aunt Caroline, "started in 1861. Father Abbot set about fulfilling the promise made by his predecessor. He called on all the neighbors hereabout to help build our new girls' school house. He had the brothers from the abbey do most of the work. He hired Mary Cahill as the new teacher and agreed to pay her fifty cents a month for each girl who attended regularly."

"Oh," said Lizzie, "I followed Miss Cahill."

"That's right," said Aunt Caroline. "She was still teaching a year ago when I started here as mistress, but she fell ill. So, Father Abbot engaged you this spring. You come with good recommendations, Lizzie. And I told him only yesterday of how competently you have been teaching. The girls are fond of you and the parents are happy."

"Thank you, Mrs. Warren," said Lizzie, blushing.

"I only wish Sally had some of your piety and docility," added Aunt Caroline a bit acidly, but she rose and walked over to me and gently patted my cheek.

2.
Starting the Order

Looking back from these years of the Twentieth Century, as an old lady now, I am impressed by the really devout and holy life we led and the sacrifices we made in the little school and cottage on Charity Hill. At Charityville, as it was often called, the poorer children paid nothing at all and only about half the girls paid their fifty cents a month.

School commenced the first of May and lasted until the end of October. That seems odd to us today in Iowa, but it was customary in the country districts of central Kentucky. That's how I had received my education as a young girl, both in the district schools and in the academy at Loretto.

Aunt Caroline, with all her austere traits, could show a winning and charming side. The girls were fond of her despite her rigid discipline. She cast enough of a spell over me to persuade me to teach a class along with mending for the boys in the monks' school. She enticed Lizzie and me to walk with her every morning. We trekked the three-quarter mile tree-lined road to the parish church for Mass and sometimes for other devotions. We grew to love it. She gradually introduced a short period of meditation along with our evening prayers at the cottage.

When I left at the end of October to return to Marion County for the winter, Aunt Caroline said, "When you next see me, Sally, I'll probably be a Franciscan nun. But please don't say anything to the Walkers or others about it, will you? I'll write your mother about it later on."

I knew that Aunt Caroline and Father Abbot had been pushing the plan which she had been quietly nurturing all year.

A month later, Ma made loud exclamations over Aunt Caroline's letter.

"Why, Sally!" said Ma. "What do you know! Caroline has gone and become a nun. Of all things!"

"She did?" I said in feigned surprise. "When did that happen?"

"Well, she went up to Louisville and made a retreat at the Franciscan fathers' church, and then--oh, I'll read it--'I received the habit of the Third Order of Saint Francis privately at the hands of the Reverend Father Dionysius, pastor of Saint Boniface Church on the 23rd of November, 1864.'"

"Privately?" I asked. "Why privately?"

"Oh, she says that it's secret only for the time being. She's coming back to Charity Hill to live in the school cottage there this winter."

So, that was that.

In the following spring, April of 1865, Lizzie Lillis and I returned to Charityville. I was both curious and anxious to see her, and only on my arrival did I learn that she had taken the name of Sister Elizabeth. She wore the Fransciscan habit and looked as austere and charmingly pious as ever.

Hardly had we started with our teaching in May when the cottage took fire during the night. In a few hours it lay in ashes. The school was damaged. So, with what few belongings we saved, we transferred to the original little brick school building on Calvary Hill, nearer to the abbey.

But I enjoyed the school year and felt we succeeded. Lizzie and I were pleased with the program of spiritual devotions Aunt Caroline had introduced. Toward the end of the school session she suggested that we also might like to become Franciscan nuns. Lizzie Lillis was very willing, but I hesitated. The idea of entering the religious life had presented itself to me before, but I had never entertained it long or seriously. The gravity of such a step now made me reluctant to come to an instant decision. So, I asked Aunt Caroline for time; I wanted to fathom my inner response to such a holy vocation and I pondered and I prayed.

When I had previously thought of a religious vocation, I had naturally visualized the convent life of the Sisters of Charity and the Sisters of Loretto. I had been acquainted with them. To me, even young as I was, Aunt Caroline's new community seemed a daring religious venture. But, I believed I had a vocation. In the Walker homestead over in Marion County, my happy young life had a background of deep piety; the Cambron and Walker families had brought with them to Kentucky the strong Maryland Catholic traditions. The habit of nightly prayers was rigorously kept and even attended by my nurse and the other Negroes of our plantation.

Starting the Order

When some time later Aunt Caroline said to me, "Now that the terrible War of the States over, God's peace is back in our land and we can do so much good for the poor girls," I finally agreed to take the decisive step.

Lizzie, older than I, had no close family connections and could make her own choice. I had to write Ma and Pa several times and visit home in Marion County. They finally gave their consent and seemed pleased. Abbot Benedict said he had prayed and planned for this a long time. Our friend, Bishop Spalding, left to become Archbishop of Baltimore and another good friend and a Frenchman, Bishop Peter Lavialle, became the new head of the Louisville Diocese. Abbot Benedict invited Bishop Lavialle to come to Gethsemane and to pontificate at the ceremonies when Lizzie and I received our habits.

Aunt Caroline tutored us. Lizzie and I tried faithfully to prepare for the great day. I was taking the name of Sister Margaret and Lizzie was to receive the name in religion of Sister Angela. The great affair, January 21st, 1866, took place in the parochial church at Gethsemane.

Pa and Ma came for the Pontifical High Mass. Much of the ceremony was strange to me, but I was impressed by it all and was serious and yet very happy. We all watched and listened carefully as Aunt Caroline (Sister Elizabeth) made her profession and as Lizzie and I were given our habits by Father Anselm. Father Anselm was the new Franciscan pastor of Saint Boniface Church of Louisville. Father Anselm announced that the Guardian of the Franciscans had granted to "The Right Reverend Father Abbot Benedict the faculties to give the habit of the Third Order of Saint Francis and to receive to profession therein" in the future. He concluded by explaining that we three ladies were not Regulars but were invested as Tertians.

What a thrill it was right after that to see the dear Bishop Lavialle himself ascend into the pulpit and to hear his eloquent sermon. He declared to the congregation that our little Order was established with his approbation and that he rejoiced to see pious persons aiming at perfection in the midst of the world. We were encouraged to hear him approve the entrusting of the female school to the care of the Sisters of the Third Order.

Aunt Caroline, with the counsel of her confessor and of Father Abbot, soon drew up an agreement, in the names of us three Sisters, to be submitted to Bishop Lavialle. The agreement stated our earnest wishes of forming a Community to take charge of the female school, gave us rights to the property and gave us the name of Sisters of the Order of La Trappe of Mount Olivet.[8]

This new name so puzzled and intrigued me that before signing I said to Aunt Caroline, "Why do we have that particular title, 'Sisters of Our Lady of La Trappe?' I don't get its meaning, and besides we refer to ourselves elsewhere as the Third Order of Saint Francis."

"Oh, that's for the future," she answered, "when we expand, as I know we will."

"The future?" asked Lizzie--Sister Angela.

"Yes, let me explain," said Aunt Caroline. "As in France and other countries where a religious Order of women is in a general way under the direction of the Trappists and is a contemplative Order rather than an active one, so we here hope later on to become Trappistines, that is, Sisters of Our Lady of La Trappe."

"But I still don't understand," I objected. "We are Franciscan Tertians, and further, since Trappistines don't carry on outside works such as teaching, what about our school?"

"Oh, that will all be arranged," said Aunt Caroline. "The outside Sisters and those having the charge of teaching the school will follow the rules of the Third Order of Saint Francis, while the contemplative nuns will take the vows of La Trappe in their special convent."

Well, we dropped the discussion then and there, and a few days later received a congratulatory note from Bishop Lavialle enclosing his letter of approbation which read:

"We hereby approve of the general plan proposed in this agreement by the signers of it, Sisters Elizabeth, Margaret and Angela, for the forming of a religious Society to take charge of the primary and work school of girls under the guidance of the Right Rev. Abbot of Gethsemane; it being understood that the Bishop of the Diocese of Louisville is to be the Ecclesiastical Superior of the Society with full power to direct its general government either by himself or through the Right Reverend Father Abbot.

Cathedral, Louisville, March 14th 1866
Peter Joseph Lavialle."

Then, Miss Julia Waters came over from Springfield to join us, hoping to be admitted to our Order. Soon other young ladies from near and far began to make inquiries about becoming postulants.

3.
Warning of Trouble

Abbot Benedict now proceeded with building the girls' school house. He sent over two brothers, skilled carpenters, to help the other workmen. A sturdy four-room school, mostly of hewn logs, rose during that spring of 1866, the "Mount Olivet Female Primary School."

With the Abbot's assistance, we spent hours with Aunt Caroline drawing up a prospectus of the school to be submitted to Bishop Lavialle.

Here are a few interesting points.

First, as a primary school, its course of instruction comprised only spelling, reading, writing, arithmetic and the elements of grammar and geography.

In keeping with the promises made by the first Abbot of Gethsemane, the school was free and without charge. Girls were admitted as day scholars without distinction of creed or religion.

Our boarding department pupils were admitted either as pay scholars or as working scholars, though all were expected to learn the common household works suited to females.

The working scholars received four hours of schooling a day and earned their board by washing, cleaning, sewing and mending, mostly for the boys' school and also for the Abbey. They worked occasionally in the gardens and by spinning and weaving.

The pay scholars of the boarding department came from the better situated families, and their terms for a session of six months always paid in advance were:

Cash or goods, $48.00
Bedding, linen if furnished by the institution, $6.00
Washing, if done by the institution, $6.00.

We couldn't have survived on the income for our work from the boys' school and the little cash from the pay scholars had it not been for the aid that came from the monks and other kind neighbors!

The bishop liked our prospectus showing we maintained a free primary school for poor girls. He didn't want us to compete with the academies at Loretto and Nazareth and other places in central Kentucky. Through Abbot Benedict he wrote to us:

"Having duly considered the . . general plan of management and regulations of your Mount Olivet Girls' Primary School to be conducted by the Sisters of the Third Order of Saint Francis, I cheerfully give it my sanction, convinced that whilst it will not injure the patronage of our flourishing Academies, it cannot fail to be a source of blessing to many daughters of our people. I hope heaven will foster your praiseworthy undertaking."

On the eve of opening school, Franciscan Father Anselm visited us. He blessed our new establishment. In the little chapel of the new house we used as our convent, he erected the fourteen Stations of the Cross. It was the 3rd day of May, the feast of the Finding of the Holy Cross. The last thing Father Anselm did before he left was to nominate Aunt Caroline (Sister Elizabeth) as Superior Pro Tempore. It was natural with her leadership and experience.

Hardly two weeks after school opened, Julia Waters came home from shopping one day, breathless and almost frightened.

"Oh, Sisters!" she said. "It's awful! I'm really afraid to tell you."

"Out with it, Julia!" I said. "What's the trouble?"

"Several of the shopkeepers," she answered, "and some of the people in their stores attacked me with arguments against our school, against our convent, even against the rules and regulations of the prospectus which they've been reading. Why, they just don't want Sisters here!"

Sister Angela, however, didn't seem the least surprised. "Remember," she said, "how Mrs. Oldham whispered of trouble when she brought her daughter to school last week? She said priests of neighboring parishes criticized our convent school, strongly opposed us, in fact. One blamed Father Abbot Benedict for our 'Mount Olivet folly,' as he termed it."

I was young and I was very hurt. And it appeared that Bishop Lavialle, on hearing these rumors, was hurt and indignant, too. He immediately wrote to Abbot Benedict:

"All opposition to the establishing of the pious Third Order of Saint Francis in the congregations under your care whether from people or clergy is unchristian and unreasonable, and only betrays ignorance and the predominance of worldly over Christian wisdom. You may read this paragraph of my letter publicly to anyone who may need it."

Another paragraph, however, wasn't read publicly. I only learned about it much later. Bishop Lavialle did not believe it was wise to give much power to Aunt Caroline as she wasn't "able of governing efficiently except in the directing of the manual labor." A clever student of human character, he had observed the dangerous streak in Sister Elizabeth. "Mrs. Warren," he pointed out, "has a proclivity for leading to the extremes of piety and that would prove injurious in the result."

The bishop was not really unsympathetic; he was prudently cautious. If more attention had been paid his prophetic warning, many people would have been spared agonizing heartache not too long afterward.

4.
Franciscan Training and a New Home

Despite ill will and strange opposition, our community grew. God certainly smiled a blessing upon our little Order. As we became known in a wider circle, so many ladies applied we could only accept half of them. Julia Waters came, then the two McGlone girls, Elizabeth Jarboe, Estella Graham, the Misses Sexton and McDonald, and Mary Finn. Five of these were from Kentucky, one from Cincinnati, one from Baltimore and one from far off Newfoundland.

And, in addition came Mrs. Mary Jane Beavan from Union County. Like Aunt Caroline's husband, her husband, a Confederate cavalryman, had fallen in the War. She had lost her considerable fortune through the War. She came for the consecration of Gethsemane Abbey, and then stayed for a retreat at Mount Olivet. At the retreat she determined to try her vocation for our Franciscan group.

Abbot Benedict joyfully observed our growth. He saw our crowded quarters with these new applicants. Also, he knew none of us had been trained according to the spiritual rule of Saint Francis of Assisi. Father Abbot talked with Bishop Lavialle, then wrote to Bishop de Saint Palais of Vincennes in Indiana. The Indiana bishop suggested he go to Oldenburgh, Indiana, to the renowned convent of German Franciscan Sisters.

Mother Antonia, the Oldenburgh superior, received the abbot with kindness and agreed our applicants should come for conventual training. Indeed, she agreed to form a separate novitiate for them.

So, our new ladies went by twos to Oldenburgh and spent the happy months of their novitiate. I wanted to go also but Providence never decreed that privilege for me.

Sisters Joseph, Gabriel, Agnes, Aloysius, Ignatius, Bonaventure, Antony, Anselm and Paula were our first trained novices. Some of them had advanced so far in their spiritual training that on the 19th of June, 1868, the Feast of the Sacred Heart of Jesus, the Reverend Mother Antonia received Sisters Joseph, Agnes, Aloysius, Ignatius and Paula to profession for twelve months. This last one, Sister Mary Paula, had been the widow, Mrs. Mary Jane Beavan of Union County. By the following 15th of July, all of them, professed Sisters and the others, returned to us at Mount Olivet. Now, reunited in the peace and the love of God, they began immediately to follow their Rule as they had done during their halcyon days at the Oldenburgh convent.

While our new nuns had been gone, we three, Sisters Elizabeth, Angela and I, had conducted the free school for girls. Abbot Benedict, burdened as he was with the heavy duties of the Abbey of Gethsemane, had also spent time, grief, labor and a great deal of money on housing for our Sisters. He wanted everything ship-shape when the nuns returned.

In the fall of 1865 Father Abbot had bought the hundred-acre Frank Smith farm about a mile from the Abbey to use for the girls' school. He had the Smith barn fitted to become the nuns' temporary domicile.

Then on a desolate wind-swept hill on this farm, Father Abbot erected the Mount Olivet convent. It was a grand and lovely project which beautified and sanctified the entire vicinity.

We watched from our windows, fascinated by the loads and loads of logs that Frank Smith and Sam Vittitow hauled to the mill to have sawed. We saw John Kister, the contractor, supervising the carpenters and tinners and painters from Bardstown. Almost every week the brothers from the Abbey applied their skillful labor. The land and the building cost well over fifteen thousand dollars, a tidy sum for those days. When Pa, Hugh Walker, called on me one day, we strolled over to see the artisans putting on the finishing touches. He told me how deeply Father Abbot had gone into debt to finish the building suitably. He noticed Brother Orsisi's skill installing the carbide gas generator, lines and fixtures. We watched the carpenters finish floorings and mount mouldings.

The frame building, one hundred by thirty feet and three stories high, seemed huge to us. It was to be heated by a woodburning hot air furnace, a novelty in 1868, and a firetrap, I realized later. The angels protected us!

A double porch, handsomely balustered, ran around the building, giving it the appearance of a large, lovely steam boat. Fifty boarders in addition to the Sisters could live there.

Franciscan Training and a New Home

When our Sisters returned from Oldenburgh and saw the subdued but colorfully painted Mount Olivet convent crowning the hill they judged it a mansion indeed!

5.
Caroline Goes to Court

Now came the most terrible and embarrassing event in my life. Now, drawing back the curtain of the years I can see the moments of drama and tragedy.

When the new Sisters returned from Oldenburgh and began Franciscan religious life according to their Rule, they wanted to elect a Mother Superior. Abbot Benedict, authorized by the bishop, presided at the election. His secretary, Father Edward Chaix-Bourbon, acted as secretary of the official function which took place on July 17th. (Years later he would succeed Benedict as Abbot of Gethsemane.) Naturally, I thought, and I'm sure that the two monks thought, that my aunt, Sister Elizabeth, would be chosen. But the Sisters, wanting someone trained in the religious life at the Indiana novitiate, elected Sister Mary Paula (Mrs. Mary Jane Beavan).

No one, not even I, at first realized what a mortal blow this was to Sister Elizabeth's pride. Of course, she was my aunt and I revered her, and my family pride was somewhat hurt too. She surrendered her authority with obvious reluctance.

Sister Elizabeth was appointed mistress of the little branch school over at Calvary Hill and, as an act of kindness to her, I was sent along. But she refused to be placated and even turned on me, suspecting I had opposed her too. Poor Aunt Caroline, so well meaning, had founded our community and school and now felt rejected, a victim of base ingratitude.

I was dumbfounded when Aunt Caroline attacked her saintly benefactor, Abbot Benedict. It was unfortunate that we three founders hadn't been sent to the Oldenburgh novitiate to learn the humility that life of a religious demands. The election could have been postponed until we had training. We were so unlearned in the ways of conventual life.

Father Jerome Moyen, Aunt Caroline's former confessor, came to sympathize and support her. Due to my confusion about loyalty to our new superior and my family ties to Aunt Caroline, Father Moyen banned me from Communion.

Pa came from Marion County to find out what it was all about. Pa was worked up both by Sister Elizabeth and by Father Moyen, and so was I. So it was decided by all of us that I should leave the Order! I returned home with Pa.

What made the rupture seem more complete was the appearance of Patience Pendleton, our Negress who, with a bundle in her arms, rushed up to our carriage and, leaping in, returned home with us.

After reaching home I heard how far the enemies of Mount Olivet had spread rumors of scandal. And, no doubt about it, Sister Elizabeth and Father Moyen had also spread reports against the Abbot.

Aunt Caroline was abetted by those who had previously opposed our convent and school. Father Benedict heard the canards calling him the architect of a plot to victimize Aunt Caroline and abolish her rights. He gladly agreed to have a new contract drawn to protect those rights. My aunt sent a copy of that contract to Pa.

"Caroline Warren, called, in the Third Order of St Francis, Sister Elizabeth, will be kept by the Sisters of Mount Olivet, to whose Superior she submits. She will be properly treated in health and in sickness and, on her side, she will do the work she will be directed to do, according to her strength. She will be dressed like the Sisters living in the world, whose rule she will follow, attending to their meetings and giving good example to the congregation as prescribed by the said rule of Saint Francis. Sister Elizabeth is assured that she will never be sent to any other house of the Order should any be established.

  Given under our hands and
seals this fourth day of September, 1868.
  Caroline Warren--Sister Elizabeth
  Mary Jane Beavan--Sister Paula,
Superior."

On the very next day a rumor was afloat that this contract was but a new trick of the Abbot! The Sisters prayed long hours in the new Mount Olivet chapel, begging God for deliverance from the ordeal and for healing of the wounds.

However, the Cambrons, a numerous and powerful clan in Marion County and Nashville, were extremely sympathetic to their Caroline. Their ancestors, and mine, John Baptist and Henry Cambron had come from Charles County, Maryland, and had settled at Cartwright's Creek in Marion County, Kentucky, in 1793 They resented any slight to family honor.

Further, friendly Bishop Lavialle died and those opposed to Mount Olivet got to the new bishop first, Bishop McCloskey. The malcontents undermined the Abbot's and the Sisters' position with the bishop. The new bishop, upset by these reports, refused to listen to Abbot Benedict. By disclaiming any responsibility in the affair, the bishop failed to terminate the scandal.

My own family unwittingly became entangled in this ordeal.[9]

A law suit was filed seeking the recovery of small sums of money Aunt Caroline had donated to our Order. Now, having severed herself from the community, she also demanded payment for her services during those years. Pa worked out a proposal to arbitrate a compromise and induced Aunt Caroline to go along.

The matter dragged through several preliminary meetings in January and, on February 23rd, 1869, the final one was held at Aunt Caroline's home. Pa was to drive over in our carriage. Since Ma, brokenhearted, refused to go, he insisted that I accompany him.

I shall never forget that day for it provided one of the most dramatic scenes that I have ever witnessed. The house was filled with lawyers and arbitrators and friends of Aunt Caroline's and the affair had all the appearances of a court trial. Judge J. E. Newman of Louisville was the only one present to represent the interests of the Sisters of Mount Olivet and Father Abbot. Mr. Hill of Lebanon and Mr. Edward Miles and Mr. Constantine Cecil had all been chosen by Aunt Caroline to "defend her rights" which Father Jerome Moyen, her confessor, determined must absolutely prevail: "The Abbot must be humiliated and Mrs. Warren must be upheld!" When Pa was called upon, he made it clear that although he was Mrs. Warren's brother-in-law, he wanted peace above all and urged that concessions should be made.

I held my breath in agony when Aunt Caroline began to give her testimony. We were bewildered by her statements. Overwrought with pique and anger, and possibly mentally ill, she went far afield with vague allegations. Finally her statements could not be understood by her own attorneys.

Her arbitrator then asked for time to make out what she meant.

"Ladies and gentlemen," said Judge Newman in effect, "we would like to bring this matter to an amicable conclusion and what I am proposing now is a legal settlement. The Sisters of Mount Olivet are making a charitable offer, far beyond what I advised them to do. I am indeed reluctant to make this offer, but I have yielded to their kind wishes. They bind themselves to turn over to Mrs. Warren the sum of twenty-five hundred dollars!"

It took Aunt Caroline's attorneys but a moment to come forward to accept this generous offer and to sign an acquittal of all charges and complaints.

I myself thought that this was a very large sum for the Sisters to pay!

Pa leaned over and whispered, "Why, this means a mortgage and possible destruction of Mount Olivet!"

Then came the most memorable moment of that dramatic afternoon. Sitting quietly behind our group had been an unpretentious but distinguished looking gentleman. He was even taller than Pa, white haired and well groomed. His name was Mr. Ben F. Mattingly, a name we Sisters were to venerate and love for years afterwards because of his great charity and generosity. A grand old Kentuckian was Mr. Mattingly and it was only later we learned that he had lost two sons in the War on the same day, July 2nd, 1863. One fell at Gettysburg fighting for the North and the younger was killed at Vicksburg defending the South.

Mr. Mattingly had risen and we all turned when we heard the sound of his mellow voice.

"Dear friends," he said, "you all know me and most of you know me well. Permit me to say that I am profoundly happy that this unfortunate affair seems to be coming to an end. I wish that my words could be the final epitaph. I have now for some time been quietly observing the Sisters and their school work at Charityville, at Calvary Hill and at Mount Olivet. I would like to say that this work for the poor female children of our districts is one of the grandest things that has ever happened in central Kentucky. I happen to know how straitened and delicate are the financial circumstances of the Sisters because of their new buildings at Mount Olivet. So, as an expression of my deep appreciation to them for their righteous and commendable sacrifice, I have here in my hand my note for twenty-five hundred dollars which I am giving to the arbitrators for Mrs. Caroline Warren, thus relieving Mount Olivet and Abbot Benedict from all financial obligations."

The crowd hushed as Judge Newman sprang up, crossed over to Mr. Mattingly and wrung his hand.

"You are a Christian nobleman," said Judge Newman.

That was the last time I saw Aunt Caroline. She soon returned to her kinsfolk in Nashville where, I was told, she led a holy but very austere life and finally died in the Lord.

Father Jerome Moyen, who had sided so severely with Aunt Caroline, was almost immediately recalled to France by his religious superiors.

I went back home with Pa.

6.
Write the Bishop Yourself

Almost every day my thoughts went back to Mount Olivet and every day I prayed to the Holy Spirit to aid me with His gifts of Wisdom and Fortitude. Pa and Ma knew I was unhappy and were very kind to me. My sisters and my brothers were keenly aware of it.

Every week we heard news about Mount Olivet. Then we heard it was to be closed and the Sisters removed. I couldn't eat.

The new bishop of our Louisville Diocese, William McCloskey, had heard all the wrong reports. He was angry, but we couldn't believe he'd take such a drastic step. I felt I had abandoned the Sisters and I must have begun to brood.

Pa called me one day and spoke to me a bit sharply.

"Listen to me, Sally," Pa said. His eyes searched me kindly. "I don't like to see you give so much time to introspection. You seem to blame yourself for leaving Sisters. I've thought a long time, and I'm convinced it wasn't your fault. You were the victim of circumstances and some contentious and ill-advised counselors."

Oh, I knew that by this time. Aunt Caroline's group and Father Moyen had used me as a pawn, young and innocent as I was. My heart now, more than ever, was with the Sisters.

"Get ready now," said Pa. "This is a beautiful day and you, Ma and I are going out for a little trip. We will spend overnight at Gethsemane. We want you to visit your friends at Mount Olivet. Let's find out about these reports the chatterers are spreading.

The Sisters at Olivet hugged me and I cried. The convent gardens seemed to glow with cosmos, hollyhocks, hibiscus, and nasturtiums. The laughter of the children was like the music of a dozen brooks.

My old school friend, Sister Bonaventure, drew me aside for a chat. (She had been Elizabeth Jarboe.)

"Tell me quickly," I begged her, "what are all these buzzing rumors about the new bishop and the closing of Mount Olivet?"

"Well, Sally," she pondered for a moment, "I'll say it's more than rumors. Bishop McCloskey, ever since he arrived in Louisville, has been hostile toward us--not to us as Sisters or individuals, mind you, but to Mount Olivet. Yes, that is certain."

"All right," I said, "Go ahead. Why? Why does he want to move you from this beautiful place?"

"Ah," she said quickly, "but he doesn't consider it a beautiful place. He says it's inland, inaccessible, and that we could never have a future here. Furthermore, he thinks we shouldn't be anywhere near Gethsemane Abbey."

"Of all things!" I exclaimed. "Why, Father Abbot Benedict is the protector and patron of this Order. You depend on the work and help of the boys' school and the monks."

"That's just the point," said Sister Bonaventure. "The bishop says if Abbot Benedict dies, we die. The new abbot may not want us. We're not Trappistines."

"That's true," I said. "They walk in silence. You teach. They live by meditation. You live by action."

Sister Bonaventure nodded. "Franciscans are activists. Father Abbot says there is so much to do in this young country. From our teaching we will clear our debts. In a few years, we will be as well established as the Sisters at Oldenburgh."

"Do you agree with Abbot Benedict?" I asked.

Sister Bonaventure laughed cheerfully. "Perfectly! Do you know that despite the gossip, despite the unfortunate affair of Sister Elizabeth, we still have ladies knocking at our door for admission to our Order almost every week? Look at the new faces you've seen here this evening. Our school is healthy. We're busy. We're earning our way. We're all confident except Sister Paula."

"The superior herself? Mother Paula?"

Sister Bonaventure shook her head sadly. "Mother Paula is all mixed up. One day she says, 'The bishop's right.' The next day she says, 'We should stay.' Then, 'We should move from Mount Olivet.' She knows the abbot's heart is in our primary and secondary schools for needy girls."

Sister Bonaventure smiled quickly, took my arm. "Let's go to Mother Paula's office. She should be coming out of the chapel now. She's been hoping you might return."

"She really has?" I asked happily. "I wonder if I would be *allowed* to return."

Write the Bishop Yourself 27

Sister Bonaventure led me upstairs to Sister Paula's tiny office. Mother Paula's face looked pale and distraught under the little gas lamp she had just lit. When she saw me, her face beamed and she threw her arms about me. "Sally dear," she said, "I heard you were here and I'm so glad to see you. Did Sister Bonaventure tell you I've been asking about you?"

"Yes, Mother," I said. "She even said that you were hoping I'd return."

"I am hoping that," said Mother Paula, "I really am. But you know, Sally, we are under the jurisdiction of Bishop McCloskey. If we remain here, I'm sure he would permit me to receive you. Under his spiritual direction we must do what he wishes."

She turned and looked out of the window. Sister Bonaventure and I stood uneasily in silence. The clock ticked in the hallway.

Mother Paula faced us again. "Yesterday," she said, "Sister Amata and I were in Louisville." Sister Amata was one of the new nuns. Mother Antonia, of the Indiana Franciscans, had gladly sent her to Mount Olivet as Mistress of Novices after Mother Paula's election. And it turned out that without that genius and darling in those trying days, we never would have succeeded,

"The bishop had asked us to come," Mother Paula continued, "to talk about moving."

"Oh, Mother," said Sister Bonaventure, "would you tell Sally about that?"

"Sit down, both of you," said Mother Paula. "You have a perfect right to hear what so concerns all of us. I don't know what to do or where to turn. I realize that the Sisters don't quite agree with the bishop nor with me. I'm glad you're here. I want to see what you think."

"Oh, Mother, we're all obedient, of course, and if he commands us to leave . . ," I said.

"But, he doesn't command us," Mother Paula said quickly. "The burden is on us to choose."

Mother Paula sighed deeply. "He says we'll never prosper at Mount Olivet. We'll do more for religion elsewhere. He again proposed to give us a farm and mission in Mead County."

"You don't mean the one the Sisters of Loretto had for a year and gave up?" asked Sister Bonaventure.

"Yes, I suppose I do mean that." Mother Paula said.

"He would move the mother house to Mead County?" I asked.

"The bishop," she said, "is dissatisfied with our state charter which names us legally as the United Schools of the Abbey of Gethsemane. Bishop McCloskey maintains we can never have an independent existence, but Judge Newman says the charter grants us the right to be separate and to have our own property."

"Senator Johnson," I said, "told Pa that Mount Olivet is an independent institution in every way except spiritual."

"But the bishop has so many other objections," said Mother Paula. "If we were Trappistines under supervision of the monks it would be different. And, forgive me, he thinks the trouble with your Aunt Caroline will hang over our heads as long as we're here.

"Finally, he repeats, when Father Abbot is gone, we leave without anything."

"But he doesn't command us to leave?" asked Sister Bonaventure.

"No, the good bishop doesn't go that far." Mother Paula shook her head. "I don't know what to do."

Driving home the next day with Pa and Ma I felt happy. My Sister friends wanted me back. Pa listened to my chatter, then suggested, "Why don't you write to the bishop yourself? I'll help you with the letter. We'll ask him directly whether the Sisters are to be sent away from Mount Olivet. And, if not, can you be received there again. Let's have an end to this uncertainty, especially for you, Sally."

I wrote Bishop McCloskey and he answered almost immediately.

"Louisville, May 17th, 1869
"Miss Sally Walker:

"Your esteemed letter of the 15th inst. was received yesterday, and I can only say that I have no intention whatever of sending the Sisters away from Mount Olivet. They are a religious community living in my diocese subject to the Bishop, like any other religious community, and they are perfectly free to receive you whenever they think fit, and so far as I am concerned, you have my full approbation to join them.

"Believe me yours most respectfully,
"William McCloskey, Bishop of Louisville."

I sent the bishop's letter with one of my own to Mother Paula and Sister Amata, and within a week I was back at lovely Mount Olivet as a member of the community. Patience Pendleton and her husband, Andrew Jackson, came with me. Arrangements had been made for Patience to do housework and Andrew to work on the convent farm.

7.
A New Name and an Old Rescuer

My probation and postulancy passed quickly. Our class of postulants received our habits in our chapel. We became novices in the ceremony presided over by Abbot Benedict. My former name in religion had been Sister Margaret, but now I received my beautiful new name, Sister Frances, I would carry for half a century.

I took over a class in arithmetic and supervised the girls at spinning and weaving.

Our community was happy again, except for the uncertainty. The bishop urged Mother Paula to move, first to Danville, later to Franklin, and again to other towns--some strongly non-Catholic. We suffered because of Mother Paula's indecision.

Then Abbot Benedict, to give us security, deeded over all the property, including the farm, to the Sisters. Bishop McCloskey objected vigorously. The abbot read his statement, admitting some virtue to it:

"As regards the transfer of the farm of Mount Olivet to the Sisters with its debt," wrote Bishop McCloskey, "I can only repeat what I said to you before, that I object to it most decidedly. I am not sanguine of the success of the Sisters' schools and if they accept this debt and fail, then the disagreeable verdict of the odium which would necessarily follow would fall upon my shoulders."

Sister Amata said to a tearful Mother Paula, "I am still confident that the institution can easily support itself by careful management."

Then reappeared our rescuer and gallant knight of old, Mr. Ben Mattingly. His home was not far from the Walkers of Saint Charles Congregation in Marion County. He was in Louisville the day Father Abbot returned from discussing Mount Olivet with the Reverend Mother Antonia at Oldenburgh.

Mr. Mattingly, hearing of Mount Olivet's predicament, gave five thousand dollars to retire Olivet's obligations.

Our joy at the convent was unbounded when we heard. The bishop's principal objection was now gone. He had recently written, "When the debt is paid, the Sisters may receive the property . . not before." We gathered in the chapel before our Lord to offer up our thanks. Then Mother Paula, along with the councillors, Sister Joseph and Sister Angela, drew up our "Certificate of Gratitude:"

"The Sisters of the Third Order of Saint Francis conducting the school of Mount Olivet,[10] Nelson County, Kentucky, wishing to testify their gratitude to their principal founder, Mr. Ben Mattingly of Marion County, promise that one pair of beads said daily by the Community will be offered up for the welfare of his family as long as the said Community shall subsist; that all the Communions made by the members of the Community on Sundays will be offered for the same intention."

A few days later there came up the Mount Olivet drive a fine team of greys driven by a fat, smiling black coachman. Out from the carriage stepped the tall, white-haired Mr. Mattingly. We spent a pleasant half-hour with him on our broad, balustered porch. The school girls came over and sang a song in his honor and we all toasted him over our lemonade and cakes.

8.
To Move or Not to Move

One novice I met on my return to the convent impressed me profoundly, Sister Jane de Chantal. She had been Mrs. Charles Batre. Widowed, yet still young, educated, widely traveled and wealthy, she was nevertheless humble and pious. I was surprised to learn she was a convert to the Catholic faith.

Sister Jane and I often took walks and she proved to be a charming conversationalist. She told me her story of how she came to such a secluded place as Mount Olivet.

"My manner of coming here and even the desire to become a Sister seems almost a miracle to me," she related one day. "My life, up to a couple of years before entering this sweet little place, was one continual round of excitement and pleasure. I lived and played in New Orleans without one iota of Catholic influence."

"Oh, yes," I said, "you were a convert."

"But not till long after I was a widow. You see, I was born in North Carolina, moved to New Orleans when I was a girl, married Charles Batre of a grand old Creole family. We weren't married in the Catholic Church as we should have been. Religion meant nothing to me in the jolly, carefree days. Then came the War. The last time I saw Charles, he was marching away with a Louisiana regiment to join the Confederate Army of the Mississippi."

"He was killed in the war?"

"At Shiloh, under General Pierre Beauregard. He was mortally wounded on the last day of fighting and died some days later. I inherited part of his family's wealth. The Union army held New Orleans, and, with the Northern officers and politicians, built a frivolous and gallant world. I was soon drawn in.

"Then God in His great mercy threw me in the way of Bishop John Quinlan of Mobile. I had gone over to Mobile with a party of merrymakers. By chance I learned from a friend of my husband that Bishop Quinlan had administered the last consoling rites of the Church to Charles in the camp hospital. The bishop had rushed in to give aid after the Battle of Shiloh. I was astonished and intrigued by this news. Since I had never learned the details of Charles' death, I called on the bishop. So kind and inspiring were his words that I changed my whole plan of life! From that moment I was a different person."

"How wonderful!" I exclaimed.

"The bishop called Father Pellier, a wise and saintly priest, who began my instructions and later received me into the Church. It was the hallowing influence of Bishop Quinlan and Father Pellier which proved to me that there was a holier and nobler aim in life than the one I had been following.

"Soon after this, I left home by myself with no fixed purpose as to where I would stop. A misdirection brought me to Nashville instead of Knoxville. Three convents denied my application on account of my widowhood and my age. All my life I had felt a holy reverence for the monks of La Trappe and had even read their history as a child. So, I came to Mount Olivet to be near the Trappists, all that early reverence re-aroused. Some might see it as chance, but to me it was the guidance of God.

"When I came, the Mount Olivet community was near being crushed by controversy. Each side tried to draw me into the plot, just as you were drawn in through Mrs. Warren. But still God guided me and I refused."

Such were the conversations of Sister Jane de Chantal--she who would later become our beloved superior.

Of different tenor entirely, however, were the new conversations going on between the bishop and the abbot and between the bishop and Mother Paula.

The bishop's chancellor and his lawyer examined the revised charter of our institution--revised because of our acquisition of the debt-free farm--and had found it faulty. Not all the assurances of Senator Johnson, the lieutenant-governor of Kentucky and of Judge Newman could convince the chancellor. At about the same time, after having had private interviews with Sister Joseph and Sister Angela, his lordship, the bishop again wrote Mother Paula urging her to establish her school and novitiate at Henderson or at Flint Island.

Mother Paula, without consulting her Sister councillors, then yielded, much to our disappointment. Especially

To Move or Not to Move 35

disappointed were those novices accepted under the special promise that they would be professed only for Mount Olivet.

The chagrin of Abbot Benedict was extreme. He was still, up to this moment, constantly and carefully building up our community and its schools. Lately he had sent over brothers and other workmen to work in our fields. He had donated live stock to our farm. Our school for the poor girls and the one for poor boys near Gethsemane were the apples of his two eyes.

However, Abbot Benedict saw a slight ray of hope for the schools. Bishop McCloskey had written him, "All things considered, I do believe that it is better for the Sisters of Mount Olivet to establish themselves elsewhere . . . I trust, nevertheless, that the schools may not be broken up."

So the abbot immediately wrote Mother Paula requesting her to leave at Mount Olivet two professed Sisters and two novices or candidates. He promised further to arrange that the Mount Olivet farm would remain forever the property of the new convent.

Startling events then began to occur.

Mr. Ben Mattingly heard that the Sisters would sell their Mount Olivet property when they established their convent elsewhere. Accordingly he wrote a statement--a copy for the Abbey and a copy for us:

"I, the undersigned, paid the debts of Mount Olivet under the specified condition that the Sisters would pray for me and my family as long as their community would subsist. But if the Sisters are to sell the property of Mount Olivet at their own will or by the Bishop's order, and move elsewhere, I expect that taking with them the five thousand dollars I paid they will fulfill their promise in their new convent or refund the money to me or my wife and children if I be dead. But if they stay at Mount Olivet, I intend to help them along every year till my death and even to make them a donation in my will because I believe it is a good and holy thing to educate poor little girls, without parents or friends, and to teach them how to love and serve God and become useful members of society, good Christians and pious mothers.

"B. F. Mattingly."

9.
The Next Casualty

The next casualty at Mount Olivet: the sudden departure of Sister Amata for Indiana. The Oldenburgh convent had affectionately looked upon our little Franciscan group as both a sister and a daughter community. And good old Mother Antonia had been happy to allow her most experienced nun, Sister Amata, to remain with us as assistant to Mother Paula and as mistress of novices. But, aware of the contention at Mount Olivet, the indecision of Mother Paula, and the hopelessness of future peace, Mother Antonia recalled Sister Amata--recalled her suddenly and overnight. We were aghast.

We said to Mother Paula, "Can't you be decisive?"

She said, "Well, yes and no."

Mother Paula, distraught, feeling helpless with Sister Amata gone, resigned as superior of our Order. This proffered resignation took zealous Bishop McCloskey by surprise. He wrote, "As Superior of the house, I naturally look to you for an explanation of so serious an affair as the sudden departure of a religious from my diocese without my knowledge. I cannot accept your resignaton and until I receive an explanation I cannot take any step in the matter."

The proposed removal of Mount Olivet was put off. Father Abbot, sore at heart, fell sick and kept to his bed for weeks. When he recovered, we wrote him of our apprehensions and our hopes of remaining at Mount Olivet. The letter, which I still have, from December 16, 1869, though it's old and crinkly, said, in part: "We, the undersigned Sisters of the Third Order of Saint Francis (who) devote ourselves to the care and training of destitute girls . . do sincerely assure the Abbot, that if we leave him and his school, it will be against our will, and we declare to him that we are not satisfied that the Bishop objected to our making our perpetual vows, and allowed us to make vows only for one year, contrary to our Rule."

The letter also said:

"We wish to accept the farm and the large new building offered to us as a payment to teach the school at Mount Olivet. We do not understand the opposition of the Bishop, who wrote . . that he would allow the Abbot to transfer us the farm at Mount Olivet, when the debts caused by the construction of the buildings would be paid. A good Catholic gentleman, Mr. Mattingly, paid all our debts, under the promise we made to say some prayers for him and his family. The Rt. Rev. Bishop saw our agreement before we received the money and gave our consent and now he is about to force us to break up our agreement with our benefactor, as well as with the abbot.

"Our Statutes, giving us the privilege not to be sent to another Community of our Order without our consent, we wish to die where we promised to stay and there to take care of our poor children as far as our means will allow us. We have no ambition, as likewise no desire to have a wealthy place and a large school; but we desire to remain poor and do good on a poor farm, forgotten and despised by the world." [11]

When Father Abbot showed this letter to him, the bishop said he would reflect on it and promised to allow things to remain just as they were until he could come to Mount Olivet.

Since Sister Amata left, Mother Paula leaned more and more upon the wise counsel of Sister Jane de Chantal. Neither Jane nor I were professed yet. Five of us waited during that spring of 1870 to be professed. But constant delays came from the bishop's absence and the inability of his administrator to visit us.

One day Mother Paula summoned the councillors, Sisters Joseph and Angela, and Sisters Jane de Chantal, Phillipa and I, to meet a priest-visitor on our broad porch. It was a beautiful spring day with the fragrance from the lilacs in our gardens pervading the air. As we looked over the balustered railing we saw our farm verdantly lovely rolling out under the warm sun toward the tobacco fields in the distance.

"This is Father McNicholas, dear Sisters," said Mother Paula, "and he has come to us with a letter of introduction from our beloved bishop, Dr. McCloskey."

The reverend father begged us all to be seated. "I am glad of this opportunity of explaining the purpose of my visit," he said. "I am from Flint Island and you will remember, Mother Paula, that the bishop spoke to you before about my place as a suitable locality in which to establish your community." He paused momentarily as he noticed us all glancing at one another, and then went on. "The bishop, as I think you all know, does not believe that Mount Olivet is the place for you, and he told me himself that he would never have approved of your coming here had he been bishop of the diocese at the time your community was started."

"But, Father," said Sister Joseph, "Bishop Spalding already in his day looked forward to the founding of a Sisters' institution here, and Bishop Lavialle so cordially approved of us and our school for poor girls being here. What would happen to our school and all the girls if we went elsewhere?"

"Oh," answered Father McNicholas, "the bishop says the school here at Mount Olivet does not require a religious community to carry it on. Neither he nor I see any danger of Olivet's school being neglected should you move to Flint Island. But our principal objection, Mother, is the poverty of this place."

Then Father McNichols launched into a long speech representing in the strongest terms our inability to do much in such a wilderness. When he had finished, Mother Paula nodded to Sister Jane de Chantal who in the meantime had been gazing out, as if in answer to the charge of the poverty of the place, at our well-kept gardens and our green fields.

Sister Jane de Chantal smiled and said with an attitude of quiet resignation, "Father McNicholas, practically all of us are convinced that Almighty God, Whose merciful hand has been so liberal to us in all our wants, will not abandon us. You speak of the poverty of Mount Olivet. What of it? Isn't that our element? Instead of being discouraged by poverty, we are given a fresh incentive, we are reanimated with the sentiments of our holy founder, Saint Francis, who cherished Poverty as his spouse!"

In no way daunted, Father McNicholas said, "Well, his lordship is very anxious for the change and he has commissioned me to convince you Sisters of it. May I make this suggestion, venerable Mother, that you and some of your Sisters come down to Flint Island tomorrow or the next day and examine the location? I think you ought to move immediately in this matter."

Then Mother Paula spoke up for the first time. "Oh, Father, we can't give you an answer to that before consulting together. This is a serious matter for us and requires consideration."

"Why, I see nothing serious in it," replied Father McNicholas. "We have consent of our bishop, I acknowledge him for my superior, and I suppose you do, too. May I repeat that I see nothing to entice you to this poor place. Why, it's so poor that it can't produce black beans!"

"Oh, yes!" said Sister Jane de Chantal. "Not only does it produce black beans, but white ones as well!" We were all amused at this. Not one of us could supress her laughter.

Somewhat fussed, Father McNicholas made his farewells and said, "I regret returning to the bishop without a satisfactory answer. I fear there is some outside influence here!"

Several days later we all agreed with the sentiments in the letter which Mother Paula penned.

"Right Reverend Bishop:

"Through The Rev. Father McNicholas I received your kind expressions of several days ago. Please accept our very sincere thanks for the interest you manifest in our welfare and prosperity. After serious reflection we have concluded that we cannot remove now, though when our number increases, if your Lordship thinks it best to remove our Novitiate, we hope to be able to comply with your wish; but for the present we could neither do that nor supply Sisters for a mission having only three professed although (we do have) a good group of novices and postulants, and taking into consideration that either step would be an injury to Mount Olivet which, to speak conscientiously, we could not abandon. Humbly requesting a remembrance in your holy prayers and sacrifices, I remain remain, Right Rev. Bishop,

"Your humble servant in Christ,
"Sister Paula."

Somehow or other we felt more secure after this and daily there were prayers and songs of thanksgiving ascending to Heaven from our chapel. Our farm yielded a fairly fat harvest in 1869 and the prospects were good for a similar one in 1870.

On April 18th we had tentatively acquired a small addition to our land. Sister Jane de Chantal, out of what was left from her fortune--like members of other Southern families she had lost much through the calamitous war--bought the little farm of Richard Vowels which lay contiguous to ours. It was for the "Corporation of the United Schools of Gethsemane." The price she paid was between two and three thousand dollars. In July, after she had finally been professed, along with six others of us, she willed this farm to the Sisters of Mount Olivet.

Then we learned that Bishop McCloskey was in Rome, taking the dispute over jurisdiction of Mount Olivet

(Trappist control from Gethsemane vs. episcopal rule from Louisville). The issue was not only being taken up by the General Chapter of Cistercians in France, but also before the Congregation of the Propaganda in the Holy City of Rome!

Whether or not it was the news that affected her, Mother Paula on July 4th tendered her resignation to her councillors, Sisters Joseph and Angela, and sent notice of this resignation to Abbot Benedict. Her resignation was accepted the following day. Within a few weeks, at her request, she was permitted to return to Oldenburgh where she had spent the happy days of her novitiate. She was only too content to escape the distractions and responsibilities of her office. The few remaining years of her life were spent in the peaceful Indiana convent, laboring and preparing for the end which was not long in coming.

10.
Controversy Carried to Rome

It seems incredible to me today that our little struggling community of nuns, whose establishment was still in its merest infancy, should have been the root-cause of an ecclesiastical dispute that reached across the Atlantic and was aired at the General Chapter of the Trappists in France and was discussed by grave old bishops and cardinals in Rome. Only a few moments on their agenda, perhaps, but we were there!

The enduring and conflicting views of two zealous but obstinate churchmen, Abbot Benedict of Gethsemane and Bishop McCloskey of Louisville, clashed at several points, but the crucial question between them was always Mount Olivet and its schools.

At Rome, attending the Vatican Council of 1870, was Archbishop Martin J. Spalding of Baltimore, a loyal and powerful friend of Father Abbot. Archbishop Spalding had been a friend of the Gethsemane Trappists of Kentucky from the time of their arrival in 1848. He was a staunch Kentuckian himself, born only a few miles from Gethsemane, at Bardstown. He was a descendant of an old Maryland English Catholic family that had come to Kentucky in 1790 with my Walker ancestors.

Archbishop Spalding was aware of the long drawn out dispute between the abbot and the bishop. He had been a friend of Abbot Eutropius, Benedict's predecessor, and had approved of Abbot Eutropius' plan of establishing free schools for poor children near the abbey as a tangible symbol of gratitude to the Kentucky supporters of the abbey.

Another friend of Father Abbot was Cardinal Antonelli and through him and Archbishop Spalding the matter was laid before the Propaganda. After a full examination, Benedict's Olivet position was favorably reviewed. The case was sent back to Archbishop Purcall of Cincinnati, the metropolitan of our Kentucky and Ohio dioceses. There the matter rested.

However, Abbot Benedict did not fare so well before the General Chapter of his own Cistercian brethren in France. The Capitular Fathers were nervous and leaned backward in order not to offend any American bishop. So we were told.

An Irish abbot, Dom Bruno Fitzpatrick, well acquainted in America from establishing a Trappist monastery in Dubuque in 1849, was appointed to come to Kentucky. He was to deliver the decision that Gethsemane Abbey and its abbot should have nothing further to do with us at Mount Olivet. The brothers were not even to help on our farm or buildings. The local bishop was to appoint regular confessors for the Sisters, since no monks were permitted to go to our convent.

But when Abbot Bruno Fitzpatrick did arrive at Gethsemane and Mount Olivet--well, that's a story in itself, to be told in a moment.

First, we made a three day retreat directed by the Franciscan, Father Bonaventure of Louisville's Saint Boniface Church. At the retreat's conclusion, in the afternoon of July 14, 1870, we professed Sisters met to elect a new superior.

On the first ballot we chose Sister Angela, one of the founding three. She refused to accept. On the second ballot we elected Sister Jane de Chantal. We prevailed upon her to accept. Later, consulting Father Abbot Benedict, our spiritual director, she appointed Sister Angela her assistant.

"Since our beloved bishop is still in Rome," Mother Jane announced next day, "I have written his administrator, Dr. Russell, about our profession, Mother Paula's resignation, about your choosing me as your superior for three years, and of Sister Angela as the new assistant mother."

"Did you mention that our farm is debt free?" we asked, "and under our control?"[12]

"Indeed, I did," said Mother Jane. "I explained that we feel bound by conscience and law not to sell or remove from here unless by the consent of the Right Reverend Abbot and his council. I added further that, God being willing, we hope to remain here always and carry on our school for the education of the poor."

One of the postulants nudged me so I ventured to ask, "How about our postulants? Will the administrator soon give them their habits?"

"I'm sure he will," Mother Jane said with a smile. "I know that Ruth Price and Francel Luckett--these two especially--

have been waiting a long time. I shall urge Father Russell to come as soon as he can conveniently do so."

The number of our probationers and postulants grew steadily all through Mother Jane's term. God prospered us and Mother Jane was a wonderful Mother. A feeling of peace and security had at last begun to settle upon the Mount.

Mr. Ben Mattingly continued to shower his princely generosities on us during these years. He bought us the three acres of land that lay just beyond the convent's confines, acres we wanted to complete our gardens. On one of his visits he surprised us by bringing a group of black workers and several loads of lumber, built porches on our old buildings and extended the great porches on our new main building.

Mr. Mattingly induced his friend, Mr. John Sexton of Cincinnati, to present us with a mandrel (axle) and circular saw and then he furnished all the needed belting and machinery. On several occasions he sent us new beds and beddings as well as furniture for the girls of our schools.

More and more poor students came to us. One day in November I was asked to show Mr. Mattingly the changes on our grounds and buildings. He remarked, "Mount Olivet ought to feel much encouraged, it seems to me, from these improvements it has undergone in the last two years."

"Yes, sir," I answered, "and these improvements are bringing their results. This last session our school was larger than ever before. And Mother Jane de Chantal is highly pleased because the girls passed such satisfactory examinations. The applicants, so far, for the next session, have already exceeded our ordinary number."

Mr. Mattingly smiled and nodded his head approvingly. Then his face became grave. "I had to tell Mother Jane distressing news this morning," he said gently. "She will soon inform all of you about the matter. Dom Bruno Fitzpatrick, the superior of Mount Melleray Abbey in Ireland, has arrived at Gethsemane and is acting as the representative of the General Chapter of Cistercians in France."

"Oh, we've heard rumors of his coming," I said excitedly. "But are the rest of the dreadful rumors true?"

"What rumors are those?"

"Why, that he is commanded to inform Abbot Benedict that he may *never, never, never* come to Mount Olivet," I explained. "And that the brothers are never to be allowed to come over here and work."

"Perhaps," he said hesitatingly, "but I'm not absolutely certain. However, Dom Fitzpatrick will be over here himself within a few days to visit you and I'll probably accompany him. You'll learn everything definitely then."

It was the very next day, Friday, the 18th of November, that Father Abbot Benedict came to Mount Olivet as though on a sad farewell visit. He heard the confessions of the Sisters for the last time and withdrew the monks from the work they had commenced on the convent property.

On Sunday afternoon, just as Mr. Mattingly had foretold, he came back with Dom Bruno Fitzpatrick. Because of our depressed feelings, I must admit I expected some kind of ogre. But we never saw a grander or more lovable monk in our lives. Well built, with a big smile, short, handsome beard, sparkling eyes, he spread a courtly kindness and dazzling verve at the same time. Mother Jane de Chantal told us later some of the details of this and his following visits.

"Dear Mother," he had said, "I had intended writing to you, but Mr. Mattingly insisted that I come here with him today. I'm glad now that I came, because if any changes were to take place, it would be said, 'The Irish Abbot did it,' and you would all have thought me a tyrant. I want to assure you and all the good Sisters that any changes I shall make will be, I hope, most pleasing to God. I must act according to my conscience and if what I do is wrong or am too strict, well, there I have my superiors. The General Chapter is above my superiors and the Pope is above all."

Mother Jane then asked him directly, "Are you going to withdraw Abbot Benedict from us entirely?"

"Father Abbot can direct you," answered Dom Bruno, "whenever you need him. Necessity knows no law. I don't ask anything that is against common sense. As your spiritual director he can assist you whenever you want him. I would rather have you write to him, though, of course. It would be unkind and unreasonable to say that the monks could never do anything for the Sisters."

"Suppose," said Mother Jane, "that the machinery in our mill gets out of order, that our railroad derailed . . ."

"Oh," he broke in smilingly, "in that case necessity knows no law."

Mother Jane then pointed to the chimney which needed repairs. Father Bruno added, "Abbot Benedict can send a monk, two, as many as he can spare."

Then, turning and bowing to Mr. Mattingly he said, "I wish Mr. Mattingly to do for this place as he has been doing.

I shall consider what you do for them here as done for the order of La Trappe."

"Thank you, Father," Mother Jane said and added laughingly, "Do you know that the monks have promised to take care of the Sisters always? We have it in writing."

Dom Bruno seemed puzzled and at a loss for an answer. Then he spoke: "All promises of nuns and monks are conditional."

"Dear Mother Jane de Chantal," Mr. Mattingly then spoke up, "Father Bruno has given us all we can expect and we ought to be satisfied. I believe that Father Abbot Benedict would be satisfied if he were here now."

Dom Bruno then asked kindly, "Are you satisfied, Mother?"

"Yes," answered Mother Jane, "as far as the will of God is concerned, I am."

Several of us Sisters showed the Irish priest about the place and he was much pleased with the location and asked to see the buildings. He visited the girls and was charmed with the "heavenly quiet," as he expressed it. As the girls sang for him when he left, he and Mr. Mattingly waved their hands to all of us.

The grace of God does work wonders and here was a good example of its working in Dom Bruno Fitzpatrick. During the next few days he reflected on what he had seen and heard. He made inquiries, he pondered and he prayed. Almost miraculously there occurred a complete change in his mind and in his heart.

Four days later, during his second visit, after he had celebrated Mass for us in our chapel, he said to Mother Jane de Chantal: "Reverend Mother, since my last visit my sentiments have undergone an entire change. The holy quiet of this place went straight to me that the finger of God was in it. You will soon have a great community here and I hope to be able to contribute to it."

Mother stared at him in astonishment and Dom Bruno continued with unconstrained emphasis: "When I visited the branch school on Calvary Hill and saw the self-devotedness of those Sisters, I thought, 'How could I take their Father Benedict from them? And if I leave the Father to them, how can I take him from you?' I think it would be a sin to remove Father Abbot from a convent in its infancy and put a secular priest over it. It might destroy it. And if Father Abbot has any idea of withdrawing from you I would command him to remain.

"Out in Iowa across the Mississippi," Dom Bruno went on, "I allowed Prior Ephraim to have missions outside his monastery walls; why not allow Father Benedict? He is the only man I know of that could have carried on the work for you. Since I've found out about his difficulties, I only wonder that he isn't in his grave or in a lunatic asylum!

"I do sympathize with Father Benedict and heartily approve of all he has done and shall so approve of it when I appear before the General Chapter in France. Reverend Mother Jane de Chantal, rest quiet. Father Abbot shall not be taken from you!"

During the following week this remarkable monk accomplished another great feat. He brought Abbot Benedict and Bishop McCloskey together and sat down with them in a friendly visit. When they separated, many misunderstandings had evaporated and a great measure of mutual charity had been restored.

Dom Bruno Fitzpatrick made his last call on us at the end of that week accompanied by the Abbey prior and in his conversation with Mother Jane he tried to do away with any prejudices against Bishop McCloskey.

"Of course," Mother Jane related to us later, "I defended our case."

Dom Bruno had remarked, "The good bishop said that Mount Olivet was the first cross he had ever met."

"If so," replied Mother, "he took the cross himself."

"I know," said Dom Bruno, "that Bishop McCloskey will be glad to be at peace with you. You have misunderstood him in some ways, too, but he will be glad to be a father to you."

"We will forgive the bishop all he has made us suffer," replied Mother Jane, "and we will gladly receive him as a father."

Then the abbey prior, on his own initiative, brought up the interesting subject of our first intention of becoming a Trappistine order. When Dom Bruno heard this, he discussed the matter at some length with Mother Jane. He was delighted with the idea and he promised that he would pray fervently for the success of the movement.

When Mother related this conversation about the Trappistines to us, she said laughingly, "We built a fine castle before he left, Sisters. Let us hope it will not be built on sand."

11.
Peace and a Word from Pa

Mount Olivet now had the grandest era of peace and holy contentment it was ever to enjoy. From Mother Jane de Chantal to the newest postulant reigned a sturdy sense of security and happiness. Abbot Benedict could now continue as our spiritual director. The Trappist brothers could help on our farm and properties. The Sisters no longer suffered fear of removal.

The new situation seemed almost too good to be true. Mother Jane received further assurance in a letter from Dom Bruno Fitzpatrick in early December 1870:

"Reverend dear Mother:
"Yes, I understood you perfectly. I do wish the Right Reverend Abbot Benedict to be always your Confessor and Superior.

"I saw clearly that you did expect his removal from the office of Ordinary Confessor and that in your deep affliction it was some consolation to hear that he would visit you four times a year.

I saw clearly your meaning when you suggested a delay in order that he might himself resign his office as Ordinary Confessor and Superior. Your reasons for this delay were valid. But now all is settled. He will, please God, continue for years and years to act as heretofore.

"I do most ardently hope to see you and all the dear good Sisters real Trappistines. Pray! Pray! Pray! God bless you and God bless all the Flock, Sisters and Pupils.

"Amen! Amen! I send you all a trillion of blessings.
"Father Bruno."

Later we saw his Card of Visitation on which the grand Irish abbot had written his message to the fathers and brothers assembled in their chapter room in Gethsemane Abbey. Before his departure for Europe he had written:

"You will pray for the bishop of this Diocese. The Reverend Father Abbot will certify with me that our interview with his Lordship was productive of the most happy results. The bishop was more than satisfied; he was delighted. You will pray for the prosperity of the schools, for the spiritual and temporal welfare of all the teachers and of all the pupils. In a most special manner, we ask your prayers for the Reverend Mother and the Sisters of Mount Olivet, and we wish very particularly to include the three indefatigable Sisters at Calvary Hill. We have seen many convents in many lands; but never have we visited a Convent that pleased us more than Mount Olivet--never have we found a Superior more fitted for her position. If the finger of God is not there, we know not where to look for it, either in America or in Europe. For the glory of God and for the benefit of the Monastery itself, we earnestly pray the Reverend Father Abbot Benedict to continue to act as the confessor of the Sisters and the Superior of the Convent."

Is it any wonder that we loved this godly churchman?

Speaking of wonders, Sister Dominica said to me one day: "Did you hear? Bishop McCloskey's coming to visit! Mother heard from him--he's coming December 20th."

"He's coming?" I asked. "Isn't that his first visit to Mount Olivet?"

"Yes," she replied. "Father Abbot invited him to give Confirmation to the girls and he answered right away. He'd be happy to be here."

On the 19th, Father Bonaventure, the Franciscan, arrived to give us our retreat. Next day we were honored by the coming of Bishop McCloskey. He walked in with Father Abbot and six other clergymen--three priests from neighboring parishes and three fathers from the Abbey. And, with them, was our gallant patron, Mr. Ben Mattingly.

Sixteen of our boarding pupils made their first Communion in the morning and fourteen later received the sacrament of Confirmation. They prepared for this reception by a three days' retreat given by Father Walsh of the Abbey. Confirmation administered, the bishop asked to see the Sisters in private, beginning with the youngest. Mother Jane assembled the Sisters and sent us to see him separately. We found his manner kind and fatherly.

Afterward, Bishop McCloskey and other clergy assembled in the hall where the pupils entertained him with recitations. One student, speaking for the group, gave a simple little speech thanking him for his visit and for graces received through him. The bishop answered in a happy manner. He spoke of his joy in finding himself in the midst of children. He said he could read their sincerity in their faces.

Then, wishing the students success in school and a happy Christmas, he gave them his benediction. After the supper we had carefully prepared in his honor, the bishop again wished us success and promised to return in the spring.

Mr. Mattingly delighted in our new cycle of peace and visited us several times the next year. On each visit he showered the struggling Mount with gifts. One time he brought fourteen pairs of blankets, a barrel of molasses, a box of tea, two boxes of candles and a hogshead of white sugar. Another visit he gave us a hundred and fifty dollars, and on another he presented the convent with twelve bedsteads and four bolts of bed ticking.

Mother Jane was puzzled this year by the number of underage applicants we received. She didn't know whether they should be permitted to make their vows. One of girls, Ruth Price, especially interested me because her father, Reason Price, had been a neighbor of ours in Marion County.

I still have the statement of her father before a Notary Public, signed and sealed:

"I the undersigned Father of Miss Ruth Price, authorize the Reverend Mother Jane de Chantal, Superioress at Mt. Olivet, Nelson County, Ky., to receive my daughter at profession.

"Reason Price"
*his mark.
"Sept. 7, 1871
"Nannie Price, Antonia Willett."

Those were happy years of profound spiritual peace at the Mount. The number of our pupils grew following the ever widening fame of our school. Our primary purpose was educating the poor, but we found the daughters of wealthy tobacco planters mingling with the daughters of the poorest renters.

As we made no distinction regarding race or creed, we also had a good proportion of girls not of our Faith. Mother Jane solved problems as fast as they arose and with her management we soon paid off the debt against our conventual home. With our community on a solid financial basis, she even laid money aside for a convent. It would be a noble structure entirely separate from the school buildings.

We often recalled Dom Bruno's pointed remark about Mother Jane: "Never have we found a superior more fitted for her position."

The bishop visited us the 1st of November as the six months term of the day school closed. The children put on two one-act plays and succeeded with a public examination. Bishop McCloskey was pleased and handed out the awards.

Yet even in those days we suffered a tiny fly in the ointment--Sister Angela's restless desire to be at the helm. Probably I was more aware of it than anyone else, because Sister Angela (Lizzie Lillis) was my old friend and fellow teacher. Sister Angela didn't entirely agree with the rest of the community, except for Sister Benedict. Sister Benedict hung on Angela's every word, Some of Sister Angela's remarks about Mount Olivet made me uneasy. Where would her strong ambition to climb take her--and us?

I usually succeeded in smothering these apprehensions. I always prayed to our Lord for blessings on us all.

At this time I had another little problem. In addition to my occasional teaching of arithmetic and geography, and presiding over the spinning and weaving, I had led the girls in songs. I especially enjoyed the Negro songs we'd heard as children. Sister Dominica conducted the singing class. One day as she struggled with little Eliza Buckingham, who couldn't carry a tune in a bucket, she said in exasperation, "Liza, your voice is just like Sister Frances'."

Of course, some little tattle tale came and told me right away.

Now, I liked Sister Dominica. She was a dear and I knew she meant it as a joke, but I was crushed. I hadn't learned the humility a true nun should have. Also I was not feeling well, under care of a doctor from New Haven and periodically taking nostrums. [13]

I rushed in tears to Mother Jane de Chantal with my tale of woe.

"Why, Sister Frances," soothed Mother Jane as she put her arm about my shoulder, "Sister Dominica loves you. She wouldn't for the world want to offend you."

"That's why it hurts so much, Mother," I sobbed, "because it was Sister Dominica who said it."

"It was only a facetious little remark which I know she regrets very much herself," said Mother. "You're not feeling your best, and that's why you're upset. Come now, Sister Frances, tell me what you would like me to do."

"I want to write home to the folks and tell them how I'm feeling," I said. "I always feel better when I do that. Would you mind if I told them about the singing?"

"No, not at all," said Mother Jane as she smiled at me. "Write whatever you wish, dear child. I'll not look at any of your letters, so feel free and easy about the matter. Please don't worry over it."

So I wrote Pa and Ma. Pa came to my aid again. I know many wonderful fathers walk this world, but I do believe that Hugh Walker was one of the most uniquely Christian gentlemen that ever lived--at least, that I had the fortune to meet. He could calm my fears and give me wisdom. Pa, as I expected, answered--the response of an honest, God-fearing, Catholic Kentuckian to his daughter who hadn't learned charity and humility as she should have. To me it proved to be the finest essay on Christian submission and meekness that I had ever read--and I've read it hundreds of times since. It came to me at the right turning point of my life and many a time have I thanked God for it and for the father who wrote it.

"September 27, 1871.

"Dear Child,

"I have received yours of the 23rd inst. Your Ma told me that the Mother told you that you might write and that she would not look at it. You should always let her inspect your letters. No Community could hold together for any length of time if free communications were allowed. If your superiors impose penance upon you, you should thank God for it. They are only helping you to obtain heaven.

"I am not capable of instructing you. Your Superiors can do it better, but I will say to you that you should have no will of your own. You should be in their hands as this pen I am writing with is in mine. I never intend to pay any attention to rumors again. If you get in trouble, try to keep it among yourselves. I don't want to hear of it. The Devil is always busy.

"You say the doctor has prescribed some remedies for you. If he can cure you, well and good. Resign yourself to the will of God. All the labor, energy and zeal that you are able to perform is due to the Community. Labor is a part of religion. When you are not able, let the Mother know your condition. She will not impose more on you than you are able to perform. I don't think I ever raised a lazy child.

"I am glad to hear that the children are satisfied with you, and if the Sister did tell Eliza that her voice was like Sister Frances she only told the truth and there is no harm in it. Not one of my children has any voice to sing as I know of.

"Your Ma and myself send our kindest regards to you and the rest of the Community; says she we'll come down in good humor next time. May God govern, protect and defend the Community is the ardent prayer of your Pa and Ma.

"Hugh Walker"

12.
The Death of the Trappestine Dream

We wanted to be Trappestines--a quiet community of prayer and contemplation! An all-wise Providence ordained that we should be an active teaching order. Young America needed schools, colleges, hospitals, orphanages and hospices for the aged. Our country seethed with millions of immigrants. These dislocated people, thrown into a strange, baffling culture, cut off from their ancestral roots, often looked to the Church for leadership. Without active Sisterhoods, including the Kentucky Franciscans, the American story would have been different.

But we tried valiantly, and quite unitedly, to become daughters of Citeaux (Cistercians) for a couple of years under the leadership of Mother Jane de Chantal. She often spoke to me of her childhood attraction to the mysticism of the monks and Sisters of La Trappe. When she learned, during her novitiate, of our original intention to become Trappestines, she joyfully looked forward to the day. She once said to our whole Order:

"When you elected me superior, I found in the records of the house that a Trappestine foundation had been approved by Bishop Lavialle, and that our Sisters were instructed in the holy Rule of Saint Benedict . . . It was there that I saw the working of God's hand in bringing me here for I, too, was always of the same mind."[14]

Bishop Lavialle and Father Abbot had undoubtedly inspired the Trappestine idea. But the Irish Abbot Bruno Fitzpatrick and Mother Jane de Chantal worked the hardest to carry it out. On Dom Bruno's visits to Mount Olivet he thoroughly discussed the Trappestine alternative with Mother Jane. The spring of 1871, Mother Jane announced that the time for action had come: "Delay will no longer seem tedious to us," she said, "if we have a certainty to look forward to."

Mother Jane penned a request to Dom Bruno to teach us the steps into the Trappestine Order. She closed by saying:

"Therefore, we humbly but earnestly ask permission to follow our former call in the name of God and for the honor of our Blessed and Immaculate Mother Mary. We address our petition to you, Right Reverend Father, and, prostrate at your feet, we humbly beg you to take proper steps as soon as you deem it best. When at Gethsemane you visited us and kindly encouraged our wish, therefore we leave ourselves trustingly in your hands as children in the bosom of a beloved Father. The two who sign themselves after my name are the two who helped begin our Society."

"Sister Jane de Chantal Batre', Superioress,
"Sister Angela Lillis
"Sister Frances Walker"

There followed the signatures of all the professed Sisters and novices.

Mails were slow in those days, but in less than two months we had Dom Bruno's reply.

His style and wording are so inimitable and individual, so florid and yet so vital that I want to give here his complete letter:

"Mount Melleray Abbey
"Cappoquin
"County Waterford, Ireland

"My dear Reverend Mother:
"To you and to every one of the Sisters and to the entire flock under your zealous and prudent care, I wish from my heart many holy, holy, holy returns of this blessed penitential season. The whole life of a Nun ought to be a perpetual Lent. At least, such should be the life of a Trappestine.

"'Then, we are Trappestines, are we?' you may ask. Not as yet, but I hope, yes, I do most ardently hope that you and your dear Sisters, will in due time, enter the great Order of Citeaux, assume the Angelic Dress of the Angelic Nuns of La Trappe and taste and see even in this life how sweet it is to live according to the Holy, Holy, Holy Rule of Saint Benedict, the Abbot of Abbots, the Master of Conventual

The Death of the Trappestine Dream 57

Life, the Pride of Italy, the Light of Europe, and the glory of the Universal Church.

"Now, as you are an American, you are surely a practical matter-of-fact woman of business.

"Therefore, listen, hearken, reflect, act and persevere. Last of all, though first and greatest and most necessary of all: Pray! Pray! Pray!

"How are you to act?

"1. Draw up a petition to your venerated Bishop, praying him to sanction your holy project assigning your reasons for believing that it is really the Holy Will of God.

"2. If the Bishop be pleased to give his sanction, you will return him thanks and pray him to finish the good work by writing to the General Chapter of our Congregation to request that the Community of Nuns at Mount Olivet may be accepted by the Chapter and admitted into the Family of Trappestines.

"You will give the Bishop the address of our Vice General thus:

"'Au Reverendissime Dom Timothe'e.

"'La GrandTrappe

"'Mortgane, France.'

"The Bishop may write his letter in English or French or Italian or Latin.

"3. You will draw up a Second Petition to the General Chapter praying the Abbots of LaTrappe to sanction your holy project and to receive you as faithful children under the beautiful canopy of Citeaux.

"I do hope to see Gethsemane and Mount Olivet once more and perhaps more than once. Come what may I shall always rejoice at the recollection of your heavenly solitude and nothing, literally nothing, that would disedify anyone.

"To you, to each, to all, to everyone of Mount Olivet I send a million of blessings.
"Ever the same
"B. F., Abbot."

With this encouragement, letters dealing with the proposed Trappestine foundation were sent at frequent intervals to Bishop McCloskey at Louisville, to Abbot Bruno Fitzpatrick in Ireland and to the General Chapter of Cistercians at La Grande Trappe in France. In her letters to the bishop, Mother Jane explained several times that the school would be continued under "outside" Sisters, or Oblates, of the Third Order of Saint Francis, who would be under obedience to the Mother of the cloistered Trappestine nuns. She quoted Dom Bruno's statement that "The heavenly solitude of Mount Olivet made it the most suitable spot for a Trappestine convent" that he had ever seen in any of his travels.

However, Bishop McCloskey, shrewd man he was, doubted the success of a Trappestine project. He evaded the issue. First, he said, he must submit this important matter to his Council; later he asked from time to time for various documents to substantiate the right of our petition. He was absent from Louisville when Mother Jane de Chantal wished to see him personally on the subject.

In Europe, on the other hand, our petition was viewed with favor. Encouraging letters and gifts of religious articles came from Trappestine convents in England and on the continent. And in France at the August 1872 meeting of the General Chapter they declared on record:

"A fervent community of religious, called Franciscans of Mount Olivet, two kilometres from Gethsemane, ask at this time to be aggregated to our Congregation, promising to conform in everything to the Constitution of our Sisters. On the good testimony of the Reverend Father Bruno, Abbot of Mount Melleray, and of the Reverend Father Benedict, Abbot of Gethsemane, the General Chapter accepts them. Only the consent of their bishop has been placed as a condition.

"Father Etienne,
"Abbe' du Desert, Secretary"

But McCloskey's consent eluded us. Mother Jane went so far as to remind his lordship how he had once said, "I believe the opposition of clergy near Mount Olivet would cease if we became Trappestines instead of remaining Franciscans."

Mother Jane asked:

"Now, Right Reverend Bishop, after six years of trials and delays, may we not hope for your ratification? By the Rule of La Trappe we are under the jurisdiction of the Bishop."

The bishop explained the delay: "Rome is slow. The Church must be slow and prudent in these matters." He said he must be "guided by them." Finally, he declared that he could give no definite answer until he had consulted his clergymen and this would take time as they were scattered all over his diocese.

And so died, in the wisdom of an omniscient Providence, our Trappestine dream.

13.
Bishop McCloskey Gets His Way

Despite the bishop's expression of pleasure over our success at Mount Olivet, we knew he was still intent on moving our mother house to some other place. We still felt the opposition of neighboring priests. Sister Angela began to show friendliness toward these dissatified, restive detractors. Others had become uneasy about Angela. When she became aware of the bishop's opposition to our becoming Trappestines, despite her former support, she suddenly swung into fierce opposition to our efforts.
"Why, the very idea!" she exclaimed several times "Don't you know that Catherine Van Borah, the nun who married Martin Luther, was a Cistercian? I'll have no part of it."
Others who saw her cordiality toward our critics and enemies became uneasy also. So, finally, Mother Jane removed her as assistant and mistress of novices, appointing Sister Joseph in her place.

At election time in July, 1873, Mother Jane de Chantal was surrounded by her three years of accomplishments. We now had a large building and two hundred and seventy acres. A substantial building had been built for workers. We had not a cent of debt. Mother Jane smilingly took the rebuff about the Trappestine project as the will of God. I never heard her utter a word of disappointment--she was a brave, prudent and humble woman who had directed us with wisdom.
Mr. Mattingly continued to act generously as our benefactor. Two months before the election, he had brought the ninety-year-old Baron Constant de Hodiamont to visit. A former nobleman of Belgium, the baron had emigrated and built a fortune in St. Louis. So impressed he was by Mother Jane and community, and concerned about our safety on the hill, he presented us with lightning rods the next day. It was an expensive installation.

We now had a record number of school children and a record number of candidates for our order. Miss Mary Mooney, a new postulant, in May of '73 proved so remarkably talented she would later become our Superior and the leader to bring us to Iowa.[15]

The morning of election day, July 19th, the professed Sisters received Holy Communion at the Mass celebrated by Abbot Benedict. We then went to our Community Room with the abbot and two witnesses, Father Edward Chaix Bourton, the new prior of Gethsemane, and Father Simon, who was our regular confessor.

The abbot, after reciting the hymn, *Veni Creator*, and one Hail Mary, read us the rules of the vowed Sisters of the Third Order of Saint Francis--what they say about the Superior's qualifications, the term of three years and so on. He spoke about the importance of a good choice made through the inspiration of the Holy Spirit. Then each Sister secretly wrote the name of her choice for Superior and cast her vote into an empty urn. When all the Sisters had voted, Acting Secretary Father Edward emptied the urn upon the floor. The abbot and Father Simon wrote down the votes.

Out of several candidates, Mother Jane had the largest number of votes but lacked one of a clear majority. Twice more we voted with Mother Jane always lacking the necessary vote to establish the majority. According to our rules, after three such inconclusive castings, the bishop as our ultimate spiritual superior must appoint our mother superior. Since Bishop McCloskey was not present, Father Abbot appointed Mother Jane to continue temporarily.

On August 4th, Abbot Benedict called on Bishop McCloskey in Bardstown to discuss the election and other affairs at Mount Olivet. The next day, Bishop McCloskey came to Mount Olivet and saw each one of us Sisters privately, then returned to Louisville to make his decision.

And a week after that, while I was walking with some of my pupils on the graveled garden walk, I met Mother Jane and Sister Angela coming toward me. Sister Angela had a happy smile on her face and Mother Jane had her usually serenely pleasant look.

"Sister Frances," said Mother Jane de Chantal to me, "I want you to meet your new Superior."

I looked at Mother Jane blankly. Mother Jane was the new superior--of course. The bishop had surely reappointed her.

"It's now Mother Angela," said Sister Jane. "She has just received word of her appointment by his lordship."

Bishop McCloskey Gets His Way 61

Mother Angela! Again I looked blankly at both of them. And then I hastened to say, and tried with all my heart to mean it: "Congratulations, Mother Angela! May God bless you in your work and in your new office. I'll be your obedient subject in Christ, our Lord." I tried hard to smile.

"Thanks, Sister Frances," Angela said kindly. "You're my oldest friend here. Let me show you the note I have here from the bishop."

I read the note: "After mature deliberation and consultation with my Vicar General, I am herewith appointing you, Mother Angela, as Superioress of Mount Olivet and I am kindly requesting you to come to Louisville on Saturday that I may see you before you enter upon your duties.

"Faithfully yours,
Wm. McCloskey,
Bishop of Louisville."

"I'm taking Sister Bernard with me," said Mother Angela, "as she will be the Assistant Mother."

Mother Angela--Lizzie Lillis! No one at Mount Olivet had known her so long, and probably no one knew her so well, as I. I should not have been so surprised at her appointment. After all, she was a woman of talents, of good education and quick, brilliant conversation.

The bishop, unable to influence Sister Jane de Chantal in his views, had found in our community a headstrong nun to carry out his ideas. From living in close quarters with Angela Lillis during several years, I had learned her tenacity of purpose. While we built our schools at Charityville and Calvary Hill, she showed fearlessness in the face of opposition. The critics of our order caused her never a twitch.

In our months of agony following Mother Angela's election, one of my consolations was Sister Jane's example of humility and obedience. Her loss in the election didn't affect Sister Jane's temper. She loved Mount Olivet and the humble work of educating the poor. If she had been re-elected, oh, how different would have been the fate of our community! She would never have consented to see the school close, though the bishop had commanded us to remove the mother-house. We knew what heartache it must have cost Sister Jane to see the end of what we had built. Through hard labor she and we had built a splendid school at Mount Olivet for the benefit of poor girls.

Now Bishop McCloskey would have his way. He had Mother Angela in complete sympathy with his views. Overnight he would remove our community and make a bitter antagonist of Father Abbot Benedict.

But, Mother Angela's almost worldly ambitions were to prove her undoing and to place the severest of crosses on our struggling order.

14.
Like a Thief in the Night

What transpired from 1873 to 1875 might well be called "a hallowed bedlam of horrendous events." Before Mother Angela passed a month in office, she wrote Abbot Benedict that the contracts Mother Jane had made with him as Abbot of Gethsemane would have to be rewritten. She added: "I consider myself bound by no contract in regard to washing, ironing and mending for the boys' school--such work is the work of servant women and should be done by such persons."

A week later Bishop McCloskey visited Mother Angela at Mount Olivet. At the conclusion of his stay, he notified Abbot Benedict that he, the bishop, was reassuming his rights as the direct superior of the Sisters of Mount Olivet.

"[The Sisters] will apply directly to their bishop," McCloskey said, "in all matters connected with the spiritual government of the institution until I shall notify you of a change. I regret that I must withdraw the permission I gave you to hear the confessions of religious and others at Mount Olivet. Father Simon I hereby relieve of the task of hearing the Sisters' confessions."

Shortly afterward Bishop McCloskey announced that Father Viola, the secular pastor of the parish near Gethsemane, had been appointed our confessor and acting chaplain. Father Viola was a dear man and we liked him, but we were saddened to hear that no longer could the monks of Gethsemane ever come again to Mount Olivet. But we heard something still more startling.

"Have you ever been to Shelbyville?" Sister Dominica inquired of me one day in October.

"No, why do you ask me?" I said.

"Oh, I just wondered," she said teasingly. "Maybe you will be there soon."

"What are you aiming to tell me, Sister Dominica?" I asked.

"Just this: I had a letter from my relatives who live near there and in it they tell me that Bishop McCloskey has bought some property near the Catholic Church and, rumor has it, that our Sisters are to take over this property."

"Sister, are you serious?" I said. "What sort of property?"

"They mentioned that it was a rather old frame house but a large one. Yes, I am serious, dear Sister Frances, and I believe from what they say that they are right in their conjectures."

Abbot Benedict, we learned, was absent for a couple of months around this time. As I remember, he had been called to visit the Trappist Abbey in Nova Scotia. During his absence the dreaded bomb finally burst. On November 16th, Bishop McCloskey read a document to the monks addressed to "The Governing Body at the Abbey of Gethsemane." Drawn by Mother Angela with assistance of her close friend and principal councillor, Sister Benedict, a daughter of the Cheshires, it began: "The council of the Franciscan Sisters of Mount Olivet after due deliberation and consultation with their ecclesiastical Superior, the Right Reverend Bishop, find it necessary to enter upon new arrangements."

All the former assertions against the foundation were repeated: that the Sisters had no home of their own since it was tied in with the United Schools of Gethsemane; that they were uncertain of their being permitted by the succeeding Cistercian abbots to remain at Mount Olivet; that if set adrift within twenty years all their labor would be lost; that they had other reasons which it wasn't necessary to assign. They demanded peaceful separation, and if a school were to be continued at Mount Olivet, it would have to be completely independent except to the authority of the bishop.

Of course, the wishes of the rest of us Sisters had not been consulted. In such a grave matter which so vitally affected our future we had hoped that Mother Angela would have listened to our voices. Certainly the majority would have preferred to remain at Mount Olivet and to carry out the original intention of the founders of our community, to teach and train poor girls.

Next day, after scarcely recovering our breath from this document, we heard shouts from Mother Angela: "Sisters! We are leaving for Shelbyville immediately!" We had heard the hoofbeats of many horses and the grating of carriage wheels on the gravelled drive in front of our house. Sisters and girls came rushing from the dormitory and the chapel.

On the great front porch stood Mother Angela like a commanding general, Sister Benedict beside her as first officer. "Quickly! We are leaving."
The peace and quiet of the convent was broken.
Some of us stood in the doorways aghast.
"Come! Get your handbags and wraps. Leave your trunks --they will be brought later!"
The confusion and consternation, the dashing in and out and up and down the stairs reminded me of neighbors in Marion County when I was a girl when we heard the booming of the cannon during the Battle of Perryville. People fled pell-mell from their homes.
All eyes were on Sister Jane de Chantal. When she walked forward, obedient and smiling, with her cloak about her shoulders, the Sisters silently fell in behind her. The drivers helped them into their carriages under the terse directions of Mother Angela.
Mother Angela selected four of us--I was among them--saying to us simply: "You will remain here to look after the convent and the school. I shall write you further instructions."
The drivers cracked their whips and the horses started off on a fast trot. They did not go by the road through Gethsemane. They took the longer and circuitous route to Shelbyville which went through Bardstown. In less than a half hour Mount Olivet had been forsaken with four lonely nuns left within its portals. The end of Olivet had come like a thief in the night.

15.
Fire!

We four nuns, Sisters Bernard, Benedict, Vincent and I, tried to maintain the shadow of an institution. Mount Olivet was now but an outpost in the solitude while the mother house was in Shelbyville. And what a mother house! We soon learned that it was a small house, really unsuitable for a convent. It contained only eight ordinary-sized rooms, a kitchen and a shed room.

"We are so cramped up there," said Sister Dominica, "and, oh! How we miss the large, airy convent we abandoned."

In order to rearrange and set this old house into shape, the energetic Mother Angela, with her assistant, made several rather veiled and furtive visits to Mount Olivet from Shelbyville. They sold our horses and the wagon. They rented out part of the farm. They collected lumber and planking from the barns and they shipped these along with other more easily movable articles to Shelbyville, not by way of the Gethsemane depot, but, again, through Bardstown. We were unaware of the fact that Father Abbot knew nothing of these maneuvers.

Naturally a school was to be started at Shelbyville to be taught by our nuns. The house being utterly too small for this purpose, Mother Angela consulted the bishop and he very prudently advised that a frame building be erected nearby for a cost of one thousand dollars.

But Mother had more ambitious plans. She represented to Bishop McCloskey that we could soon have a successful and fine paying boarding school for young ladies serving the entire Shelbyville district if a large and more substantial building were erected. The bishop finally yielded to her persuasions.

As a pleader, Mother Angela was both clever and brilliant and a brick building was constructed in the spring of 1874 at a cost of eight thousand dollars--six thousand dollars of this was borrowed by Mother from the German State Bank in Louisville.

Meanwhile it became apparent to all of us that Mother Angela wished to close the school at Mount Olivet and remove us remaining four Sisters from there. To this the bishop was strongly opposed. He had given his word of honor that although he wished the removal of the mother house and novitiate to Shelbyville he favored the continuation of the school for poor females at Mount Olivet.

We who knew Mother Angela and her determination were rightfully apprehensive that she would circumvent the bishop. Abbot Benedict wrote pleadingly that the school should be continued and that he would make any sacrifice required for its support. Mother Angela wouldn't even answer his letters.

In January, 1874, Mother Angela at last wrote the abbot admitting that by our abandonment of Mount Olivet we had lost our claim on its lands. But she demanded the money Sister Jane had contributed to help buy the farm.[16] She also called for the eight hundred dollars Jane had loaned and which was payable to the United Schools of Gethsemane.[17] She concluded with an answer to Abbot Benedict's pleading to keep the school going. She said, "We'll teach the Mount Olivet School, but we cease to regard Mount Olivet <u>as ever having been a home</u>. Nor will we acknowledge it as the <u>place of our foundation</u>." She heavily underlined these phrases.

Today I marvel at the resignation we all showed Mother Angela's whims. The obedience we paid to the bishop was another thing--that was part of our holy duty. But why didn't we insist on participating in her decisions? We prayed, of course, that her leading would reflect the will of God.

We ached for Abbot Benedict because of the ingratitude Mother Angela showed him. She knew the school for poor girls had been the dream of his life. We owed our very existence to Father Abbot. He had been a father and a friend of the Sisters. And now when the school succeeded after Herculean effort, it seemed a cruel thing to abandon it.

The abbot showed great patience. Since the money given by Sister Jane de Chantal was willed to the the United Schools of Gethsemane our claim was doubtful. He would pay if Mother Angela would turn over the deed to him, but this she refused to do. The dispute continued and became acute.

Meanwhile the new brick building at Shelbyville was found to be poorly constructed. Three stories high and without a basement, it was inconvenient and unsuitable for either a school or a convent. With no stairways inside the building, we had to climb outside in snow and rain.

As a boarding school it failed from the start. The few Catholics in Shelbyville, most of them indifferent, gave us little support. The Methodists and Presbyterians each had a successful boarding academy. Our Sisters soon found they had plunged into debt with little prospect of increasing income.

Mother Angela became increasingly anxious to obtain the money she demanded from the abbot. She now made additional claims for past debts which she alleged were owed to the community. She first threatened to appeal to Rome. Then she threatened to bring suit in the civil courts against the abbey, quoting the bishop's permission to do so. The bishop soon backed out on this, but he wrote to the monks requesting they settle "the full legal claims of these defenseless women."

The monks immediately showed the bishop there were no legal claims and Prior Edward sent an additional note saying: "My Lord, having been cashier of the Abbey since the very foundation of Mount Olivet, I can certify and swear that all claims for work have been duly paid to the Sisters, and I can further prove the fact by our monthly and yearly settlements signed by both parties."

The bishop, now convinced, learned that a settlement could be made. The monks would refund the money for the Elizabeth Batre farm providing the deed was delivered. Poor Sister Jane de Chantal had been willing to sign this deed all along. So, reluctantly, Mother Angela and Sister Benedict appeared at the abbey with signed deeds and quit-claims. Father Abbot wrote a check for the amount Elizabeth Batre, later Sister Jane, had originally invested in the United Schools of Gethsemane.

During these long proceedings we Sisters were kept mostly in the dark. Mother Angela continually tried to persuade the bishop to close Mount Olivet School. "It isn't wanted by the neighborhood," she said. "Troubles in the tobacco districts nearby are growing; the school is in danger because of the night riders and Ku Klux Klanners and the Negroes." But, to these arguments, Bishop McCloskey turned a deaf ear.

The first of June, a beautiful afternoon, Lieutenant Governor William Johnson arrived to visit his niece, a paying boarder at our school. When he was leaving, Sister Bernard[18] and I walked down the road with him to his carriage. He smiled at us and asked, "How are things going? You seem to be under-staffed a bit now, aren't you?"

"Oh, yes, in a way," said Sister Bernard. "We have Andrew Jackson Pendleton and his wife, Patience, and two other good Negro women to help us and we get along quite well."

He paused a moment while he tapped the spokes of his carriage wheel with his cane. "I'm going to Bardstown now," he said. "It's a grand day for a drive. I'm to see Father Abbot Benedict about recording deeds and other business of this place. Do you have any message?"

"Yes, indeed," we both answered. "Give him our warm regards and tell him we pray for him every day."

The lieutenant governor looked at me and laughed. "I'll probably see Hugh Walker there tomorrow giving a speech at the political meeting! I'll tell him you're looking well, Sister Frances."

That same evening after nightfall Mother Angela and Sister Benedict arrived at Mount Olivet. We talked pleasantly and listened to the crickets and cicadas in our garden. A quiet, lovely night it was, a lull before the tragic storm that would blast our good name for years to come.

At midnight I awakened to screams and the shouts of "Fire!" I smelled the pungent odor of smoke. I dressed in a trice and dashed into the corridor. There I saw Sister Bernard rushing toward the bell ropes. She clanged the little convent bell fiercely through the June night. I helped lead all the girls outside and there stood Mother Angela and Sister Benedict watching the neighbors gallop up on horses and mules. Some of the brothers and workmen rushed over in the abbey cart and climbed out with axes and a ladder. A bucket brigade brought gallons of water to splash on flames. The smoke billowed black, the heat died down. Heat under the roof did a fair amount of damage, and smoke did more, but the fire finally extinguished.

Then we found Mother Angela and Sister Benedict surrounded by a group of excited neighbors asking about the cause of the fire. The two Sisters told a breath-taking tale of seeing two intruders climbing up over the roof of the porch, rushing through the girls' dormitory and going into the chapel, pouring out chloroform, setting fire to the May altar, slipping out through a chapel window and escaping at full speed in the dark. Mother Angela even pointed out a couple of Protestant gentlemen as suspects.

Naturally the Protestant men were furious and soon threatened to file a lawsuit against Mother Angela. The suit was narrowly averted by the efforts of Judge Newman.

Fire!

Squire L. P. Clement of Washington County came the next morning to take his daughter home. He offered his services for pursuing the accused with his bloodhounds and friends, but Mother Angela would have none of it. The excitement was so great and the stories so inconsistent we met neighbor after neighbor coming to see for himself.

After Mother Angela had returned from a quick trip to Louisville to inform the bishop of what had happened, we were visited by two of the neighboring pastors, Father Viola and Father Edward Crury. Father Viola's written statement, a notarized copy of which was sent to Rome, frankly summarized the tragic affair:

"The rumor spread out in my Congregation that somebody had made an attempt to burn out Mount Olivet Convent, situated in the boundaries of same Congregation and occupied by a few Sisters of the Third Order of Saint Francis and their pupils.

"At first, I noticed that every person who had been to the scene of the attempt and conversed with the Sisters gave a different account of the occurrence and the discrepancies were bearing on points very important. The Sisters were made to say, they knew who had set the house on fire. Others said they knew not who had done it. They had seen one incendiary, several incendiaries, and they had seen none, etc.

"On going to the place, we were received by Sister Angela, the Mother Superior, and Sister Benedict. They took us to the chapel on the second story of the building and showed us the damage done by the fire. Their narration and the circumstances forced us to believe, all at once, that what they were telling was false, impossible and ridiculous. I noticed contradictions in the Sisters' statements and this, all at once explained to me the reason of the various stories that were circulating abroad.

"I was then firmly convinced that whatever might have been the origin of the fire, it was not the work of an outside incendiary. This has been and is the general belief of the Community, especially of those who took the least pain to examine it."

Mr. Sylvester Rapier, a Protestant gentleman and always a loyal friend of Mount Olivet, was a little more pointed in his statement:

"After the Sisters had given their account of the manner in which it was set afire, they appeared like they thought that I did not believe what they were saying and tried to convince me that it was set afire by an outside incendiary.

"But taking everything into consideration I think that it either caught fire by some light left on the altar--which they said positively was not the case--or was set afire by themselves. It seems to be the general belief of the neighbors and of every person whom I have heard speak of it, that it was fired by the Sisters Angela and Benedict who occupied that part of the building at the time."

There was now nothing else to do but go to Shelbyville to live after that. Mother Angela had won over Bishop McCloskey. The school at Mount Olivet closed.

16.
Mother Angela

We saw Mount Olivet through to its melancholy finale and climbed aboard for the thirty mile trip to Shelbyville. The Sisters welcomed us with warmth and tenderness. They were praying in the chapel for our safety when we arrived. Sister Jane de Chantal and Sister Dominica took me about to show me the two buildings.

"Our Lady of Angels," said Sister Jane, "the name now of our Mother house, our novitiate and our school--I rather like the title, don't you? And tell me about the children-- how did you leave them?"

"They were all well despite the fuss and excitement," I said. "I really believe they enjoyed the excitement of the fire. Those living nearby went home the next day. The other girls from a great distance we left with neighbors until we could send them home. Patience and Andrew Jackson went back home to Pa on a mule they borrowed from Major Calhoun."

"You left Sister Benedict to look after affairs?" asked Sister Dominica.

"Yes," I said, "but she'll be back shortly. It was amusing while she was in charge. They had a group of men guarding the place each night as though they were afraid of night raiders. The men guarding us made so much noise we wished they'd leave."

"Did you get to see Father Abbot Benedict before you left?" asked Sister Jane de Chantal.

"No," I said, "I'm sorry to say we didn't. But we did meet Baron de Hodiamont, the old Flemish nobleman. He came over to look at the lightning rods once more and offer his consolation. He wanted to assure you, Sister Jane, he paid off Father Abbot's debts--money he had borrowed to refund your gift. He has even settled all other debts of Gethsemane. He knew you were against making such demands. But, anyway, it's all settled.

"May God reward him!" exclaimed Sister Jane with tears in her eyes. "I am so happy for dear Abbot Benedict's sake."

"Then the baron went with us," I continued, "as we made our final visit to the graves of our Sisters. He was too feeble to kneel on the grass, so he leaned on his cane and joined in our prayers." Then I described how Sister Bernard had led us in a farewell to the little cemetery. There rested the remains of the three young Sisters who died during our years at Mount Olivet--Sister Joseph, Sister Agnes and our novice, Sister Beatrice.

"Those three saints in heaven," said Sister Dominica, "are now praying for us in our trials."

We soon realized the trials Sister Dominica referred to. We conducted a parochial school for a handful of children. The few Catholics in town saw our effort as a passing fad and gave but meager support. The few dollars we took in as tuition and fees vanished. Then the money we had demanded from the Mount Olivet property melted away. We went deeper and deeper into debt for the very necessities of life.

Yet, even in the midst of our difficulties the loveliest daughters of Kentucky came to our Shelbyville portals seeking admission into our humble Order. Mother Angela, despite all her eccentricities, could show people her winning side. She was zealous and fearless for the Lord in her own individual way. And she was industrious. With all working loyally and charitably, we were able to display a brave front to the world.

Among those who came in 1874 and 1875 was Mary Mooney who had come too young to Olivet and after a few months was called home. But, after obtaining her mother's reluctant blessing, she returned to us at Shelbyville. As Sister Agnes she would become renowned as leader of our community. Another who came was twenty-three-year-old Julia Mattingly, related to our benefactor Ben Mattingly. She came from Saint Mary's near my home in Marion County and would later become our beloved Mother Mary Magdalen.

With desperate eagerness, we took our first mission school at Chicago Hill (part of Chicago, Kentucky). We needed the income. We sent four Sisters from our crowded house to teach Saint Clare's Academy with Sister Bernard[19] as superior. She was still young, but zealous and efficient, the daughter of Reason Price.

Two months later we received two parochial schools in the city of Louisville--Saint Cecilia's and Saint Bridget's.

Both of these schools were good establishments and were well patronized. Because of the demand we sent novices along with professed Sisters to teach.

But, in two years our Sisters were withdrawn from both schools, due to mismanagement and misunderstandings between pastors and superiors.

Interest on our debts ate up most of our income at Shelbyville. Mother Angela traveled about to see if friends would aid us--to stave off disaster. To save expenses she even rode on freight trains.

In August of 1875 Bishop McCloskey came to give the holy habit of Saint Francis to seven of our postulants. Mother Angela described our crisis and secured permission for a short begging tour in the city of Louisville. With a Sister companion she collected two hundred dollars--a doubtful success and a bad precedent as it began a series of unfavorable begging trips.

Then Mother Angela became the object of a threatened lawsuit. Always the lady with the sparkling conversation and clever tongue, she made sharp remarks against a prominent Catholic woman. Bishop McCloskey became alarmed when he heard the details. He urged Mother to take a companion and go to the Sisters of Mercy in Saint Louis until he notified her to return. But to the dismay of the bishop she was back in Shelbyville in a week.

The worried bishop, now thoroughly aroused, angrily commanded her to go to Cincinnati. This she did, but only long enough to call on Archbishop Elder and vent her spleen against her friend and patron, Bishop McCloskey, turning even more bitterly against McCloskey than she had against Father Abbot Benedict. She appealed to the Archbishop to protect her against the bishop of Louisville who, she charged, had forced her to abandon Mount Olivet and was now persecuting her!

When Mother Angela returned to Shelbyville she spurned the bishop's advice and defied his authority. Then, accompanied by her friend Sister Benedict, she departed from our Community forever.

The mysterious change in Mother Angela's character in the last few years had puzzled and pained me. Her sudden departure left me somewhat desolate, for I loved Lizzie Lillis. She and I had humbled ourselves before our Lord Jesus Christ in our early, embryonic Order. Along with her dangerous whims and fierce stubbornness, she had virtues of finest gold. Here I was--and here I am--the only survivor of the original founders of our community.

Through mutual friends, I found that Sister Angela went to New York and joined a group of Italian Franciscan nuns who were looking for an English teacher for their schools. She accompanied them to Rome and became a zealous and prominent member of the Order. This Order opened a mission school in Constantinople, Turkey, and my last news of her was that she was a successful mistress of novices in the Constantinople convent. I was finally consoled.

17.
Mother Teresa's Crisis

In November, 1875, Mother Angela fled and Bishop McCloskey hurried out to Shelbyville.[20] He appointed Sister Teresa (Ella McMahon of Cincinnati) superior. Reluctantly she accepted office, but we were happy with her.

One day as we put up new window shades in the school rooms, Sister Evangelista said, "These gifts of Bishop McCloskey--I don't know what we would do without them."

"I don't know what we'd do without Bishop McCloskey," said Sister Dolorosa from the top of the ladder. "Practically everything needed in the school and convent lately has come either from him or from our Shelbyville pastor, Father Mertens."

"Father Mertens sent us the basket of food for Christmas," I chimed in. "And Mother Teresa said the bishop refilled all our grocery shelves with his own money twice since New Year's."

"I do believe," said Sister Dolorosa as she stepped down from the ladder, "since Mother Angela left, the bishop is a different person. He's become so kind and generous with us."

From this time on, Bishop McCloskey did show us a different face. Exiled as we were, stranded in Shelbyville where income was scarce, we became objects of the bishop's pity. Years later he talked of his attempt to be fair to both sides when he first became bishop. He was sorry he had favored the cranks among the clergy who opposed our community at Mount Olivet. He had been misled by the advice of Mother Angela and others. Now, he said, he wanted to make amends.

We often wondered at the bishop's patience. As the years passed he met our needs again and again from his own purse. Our sisterhood barely survived. But his help, generous as it was, may have been too little, too late.

From the time Mother Teresa began bill collectors hounded us. Our trickle of income paid interest on debts. We faced starvation or closing.

We borrowed what we could to buy meal for our daily cornbread and mush. We picked up coal along the train tracks.

The bishop saw we were on the edge of disbanding. Except for his charity we would have. He paid grocery, dry goods and fuel bills and, when worse came to worst, he paid the interest on our eight thousand dollar loan.

Father Mertens befriended us as his slender income permitted. But he was moved to another pastorate in the fall of 1877.

Despite defections, our community now numbered eleven professed sisters, eight novices and a like number of postulants. Our one mission school at Chicago Hill with five sisters barely eked out a living for them. Nothing they took in was left for the mother house.

In the spring of 1877, Mother Teresa went to our old friends of the Franciscan convent at Oldenburg, Indiana. She took with her Sister Jane de Chantal, for no one was held in higher esteem by the Oldenburg community. They had been impressed by her as a student and as our mother superior. The Indiana Franciscans, however, couldn't give us financial aid. Also they had been upset by the exaggerated stories of our abandonment of Mount Olivet and of the actions of Mother Angela Lillis. So, Mother Teresa and Sister Jane returned empty-handed.

Then Mother Teresa proposed a daring plan: Return to Mount Olivet as soon as possible! "Bishop McCloskey is different now," she argued. "Father Edmund Drury, the pastor of our mission school at Chicago Hill, will now take us back."

Mother Teresa wrote several notes to Father Abbot saying the sisters had left their original home without their consent and wanted to come back to carry on their work. She said to us, almost poetically, "There at Mount Olivet stand our lovely buildings. There they languish on a lonely, wind-swept hill, unoccupied and ready to welcome us, their darkened windows ready to be lit when we cross the friendly thresholds. There our community made an honest living. We weren't forced to beg for bread!"

Father Drury did his part and tried to negotiate between Mother Teresa and Abbot Benedict. But the abbot was apprehensive. He neither wanted to open old wounds nor suffer any new humiliations. He was embittered, he said, by the unjust abandonment of Mount Olivet. He would have the school and even the mother house, but only on conditions so exceedingly stringent we couldn't accept them.

Mother Teresa's Crisis 79

On a cold day at the end of November, Bishop McCloskey hurried over to Our Lady of the Angels to have the long-awaited profession ceremony. The eight novices had waited long past probation. We even skipped the customary eight days' retreat before the vows. Our novices had from seven o'clock in the evening until six o'clock the next morning to prepare themselves for this solemn act. The bishop heard their confessions. During Mass the next morning the novices pronounced their vows and received the black veil from his hands.

Afterward Mother Teresa spoke with the bishop in detail about our wretched finances. Among other things she told him our Sisters needed winter underclothes.

"Mother," he said, "get everything necessary and send me the bill."

But this afforded only temporary relief. If it had not been for the patient forbearance of the Protestant merchants of Shelbyville who continued to give credit to the sisters, waiting years for payment, the convent would surely have closed!

Now in the darkest weeks of our history, Mother Teresa, utterly discouraged and not knowing which way to turn, called on the bishop.

"I want permission to leave Shelbyville," she said, "and enter another convent."

He put his head in his hands, shaken by this sudden request. "Please be patient." he said. "Reflect on it before you do such a thing."

Mother Teresa, exhausted under the strain, her patience used up, returned from the bishop's office to Our Lady of the Angels. She summoned all of us to a conference in the drawing room. She told us she'd asked to quit the Order and appealed to us to leave with her. She promised to provide for those who would stand by her. She knew, because of our suffering, that a number of the sisters sympathized. She looked from person to person in our group--looked us straight in the eye and asked each of us individually to come with her. I saw a number of our sisters waiver.

Even Sister Jane de Chantal, my rock of spiritual security, stood up to say a few words. She had been sitting on the bench by our old battered piano. In her agitation, as she arose, her veil swept music sheets to the floor. I picked them up and handed them back to her. Stephen Foster's popular song titles stared up at her as she re-arranged the sheets on the piano: "Old Folks at Home," "Come Where My Love Lies Dreaming." And, on top of those, in large letters, lay "My Old Kentucky Home."[21] She glanced at these and then turning she looked at me and flushed. She sat down and spoke not a word.

"How can we," Mother Teresa asked, "go on living as we have for months on corn bread and lard gravy?"

Sisters Cecilia, Veronica and Antonia arose and agreed to leave with her. Mother then dismissed the rest of us and the four sisters quickly prepared to leave. They packed, even taking things they'd contributed from their homes. I saw the coachmen carry out seven trunks to the two carriages.

It was getting dark at seven o'clock when Bishop McCloskey suddenly stepped up to the door. He had raced out from Louisville, upset over Mother Teresa's attitude in his Louisville office.

"What can I do?" he asked.

Mother Teresa, already near the door, threw her cloak about her shoulders.

Bishop McCloskey asked us to assemble in the drawing room. Hardly had he begun to speak when Mother Teresa arose and dramatically requested to be relieved of office. This the bishop granted without discussion. She then abruptly left the room followed by her three supporters. A minute later we heard the carriage wheels grinding in the gravel as they drove away into the night.

We stood there quietly; the bishop with bowed head looked grave and sad. A black cloud hung over our group. But then he looked up and invited us to go to the chapel with him for benediction. We could smile again as our voices rolled heavenward along with the incense before the Eucharist during the singing of the *Tantum Ergo*.[22] I do believe that everyone of us gave thanks to be alive and part of the Order. Our backs may have been to the convent wall, but we had passed through the most perilous trial of our lives. The strong Hand of Providence held us together.

Of the sisters who departed on that dark night I know that two were later received at Nazareth, Kentucky, and persevered as Sisters of Charity. Mother Teresa, as Miss McMahon, went to Denver and for thirty years taught and served as superintendent of the public high schools of Colorado.

In the summer of 1908 Mother Teresa returned, and our council accepted her humble petition to re-enter and die in our order. She again took up the duties of the religious life. After a few years of zealous and edifying labor, she passed on to her eternal reward. We remembered again the infinite patience and mercy of God!

18.
The Chicago Hill Schism

Bishop McCloskey appointed Sister Dolorosa temporary superior. The election, scheduled for February, 1878, failed because the casting of three ballots resulted in no majority. The bishop appointed Sister Evangelista who served only a few days and resigned. Then he appointed Sister Dolorosa who declined after a few days.

In March Sister Agnes Mooney, young enough to look like a college student, accepted the role of Mother Superior. On the advice of Bishop McCloskey she chose Sister Magdalen as assistant and Sister Dolorosa as consulter. This selection of Mother Agnes was, as it turned out, about as wise as any that could have been made. For over twenty years she was to guide our community with firmness and with, I might add, as much prudence as could humanly be expected. She would later lead us from the tempestuous and starving years in Kentucky to the great era of peace and prosperity in Iowa.

From the beginning, Mother Agnes had to deal with our poverty, a rebellion over her appointment, and a psychotic pastor. I wish I could find a more polite term, but the Sisters of Saint Clare's Academy, Chicago Hill, did rebel and resist for two years. Then came the affair of the erratic pastor of Shelbyville--poor, semi-demented Father Daly. The affair ran on for over twelve long tortuous years.

First let me tell you of the Chicago Hill trouble. We at Our Lady of the Angels humorously referred to it as "The Great Western Schism." They were good, self-sacrificing Sisters at Saint Clare's, all five of them, but they became convinced that young Mother Agnes had been illegally or unconstitutionally appointed as superior.

The effect was a bomb-shell when Mother Agnes read to us senior professed Sisters the first Chicago Hill letter.

"Dear Sister Mary Agnes:

"We were in hopes that you would become aware of your false position without our being obliged to inform you. While our hearts are full of esteem and affection for you personally, we cannot have respect for you officially.

"Our Holy Rule, with which Rome alone can dispense, expressly requires that the consent of each professed member must be asked for the valid profession of any novice. In your case the consent of the professed members of our community was not asked. Therefore we cannot recognize you as a member of our community. We are grieved to inform you of this, but we feel bound in conscience to do so."

There was considerably more in the same vein and the letter concluded:

"Trusting our dear Lord will soon deliver our community from the wretched conditions into which it has fallen we are most sincerely,

"Yours in Christ,
Sister M Bernard
Sister M Dominica
Sister M Vincent
Sister M Evangelista
Sister M Angelica"

Mother Agnes, aghast, sent the letter to the bishop. McCloskey, perplexed over the matter, wrote the Saint Clare Sisters a fatherly letter to quiet their qualms of conscience. But all to no avail. Months later they wrote asking me as the senior member of the order and a founder of the community to take note of their indictment of Mother Agnes.

"The Council of Trent," the Sisters said, "tells how Abbesses and Superiors of any name are to be elected and who are eligible to such offices." They said, quoting chapter and verse: "'An abbess, Prioress or by whatever name a Superioress or one in authority may be designated, must be chosen of no less than forty years of age, and who has lived praiseworthily eight years after making her profession.'"

Of course, Mother Agnes was too young to have been professed for eight years, was certainly not forty years old and claimed she had never heard of such a Rule.

I showed the letter to Sister Jane de Chantal.

The Chicago Hill Schism

"I am amazed," I said, "to think that the Sisters at Saint Clare's would dare to appeal to me. I am going to give this letter to Mother Agnes."

Sister Jane laughed gently. "Don't be so scandalized, Sister Frances. I received the same letter and I've already given it to Mother. It may turn out to be only a tempest in a teapot."

"Do you think so?" I asked, my indignation somewhat abated.

"Well, at least I hope so. You see, they wrote me too, because I am now the only former superior of our order. While we were at Mount Olivet, Sister Bernard, who seems to be the leader of the little revolt, was co-operative with me. Now she appeals to the two of us as senior members and pillars of the community."

"But, Sister Jane," I said, "who among those Sisters at Saint Clare's knows about the Council of Trent and its decrees about abbesses and superiors? I'm sure little Sister Bernard has never done such research."

"You're right," said Sister Jane. "Father Edmund Drury, knows Canon Law and has been advising the Sisters. Since we opened the school at Chicago Hill he has been their friend and supporter. We realize now that his influence is behind them in their stand against Mother Agnes. As for the Council of Trent and its decrees about elections, that has nothing to do with us."

"It hasn't?"

"Not at all," explained Sister Jane. "That doesn't refer to us simple religious--to members of the Third Order of Saint Francis.[23] The bishop's secretary has already assured Mother Agnes. Those decrees refer to those religious bound by solemn vows--nuns in the strict sense of the word. We are simple religious."

I was relieved, but the embarrassing revolt reached such defiance that everybody in our part of the country seemed to have heard about it. We traveled the road to Louisville many times, taking our troubles to Bishop McCloskey.

Mother Agnes said that one day the tired, perplexed bishop exploded to his secretary, "Heaven knows . . . these Franciscan ladies bequeathed to me by my predecessor are brave, zealous and pious, but I doubt if any bishop in Christendom has ever had the embroilments and contentious disorders of a Sisterhood . . thrust upon him as I have had with them!"[24]

"But, Father," Mother Agnes had said to the bishop's secretary, "what action do we take?"

"Nothing at the moment," the secretary said. "He advises you to leave these dissatisfied Sisters to themselves until they see their mistake and submit to your authority."

"And yet," asked Mother Agnes gently, "aren't they really rebelling against the bishop instead of me?"

"How so?" asked the reverend secretary quickly.

"The bishop was the one who appointed me," answered Mother Agnes. "He appointed me legally and morally, and he did so with full knowledge of all the facts in the case."

The secretary nodded in agreement, then threw up his hands as though he and the bishop were helpless.

The Sisters at Chicago Hill, however were not so helpless.

Once again our affairs went to Rome! Under advisement of the respected Father Drury, Saint Clare's appeal went to the Roman Propaganda.

Cardinal Cimeoni, agitated over the now notorious affair, wrote Archbishop Elder of Cincinnati. The upshot of it all was that Saint Clare's rebellion succeeded.

In a spirit of pious boastfulness Sister Bernard wrote in defense of her actions to Bishop McCloskey:

"Seeing no remedy near us, we had what might perhaps be called the boldness of submitting our case to the Vicar of Him Who said, 'Suffer the little ones to come unto Me and forbid them not.'. . could we help believing that the day was near when the community would be wrecked and scattered?"

And, as though with dark premonitions, Sister Bernard added:

"How near that day may be your Lordship knows best."

We felt their rebellion had triumphed. It got under our skin the way they informed us that "God in His mercy had heard their prayers and given them the blessing of admission among the Sisters of the Poor of Saint Francis in Cincinnati." They said:

"If we have erred our error has not been shown to us and we do not believe that good Archbishop Elder would fail to point out to us our faults if he could find them. Our hearts are full of joy and peace and gratitude and love of God and we love you still, dear Sisters, and if there is one shadow o'er us, one sad thought in our minds, it is that we must say farewell and leave you to toil on oppressed with troubles amid which we conscientiously feared to hazard our souls--but do not be discouraged. Trust your God!"

"Cleverly sweet, little Sister Bernard," said Sister Dolorosa to us when she read this. "She judges herself another Teresa of Avila."

However, Sister Bernard didn't win totally. Only three of the nuns went with her to the Sisters of the Poor.

Sister Dominica, grieved over the part she had played in the rebellion, wrote Mother Agnes a humble apology and begged to come back. Mother Agnes talked with us and then let her come. Sister Dominica returned to us at Shelbyville and remained loyally with us until the day of her edifying death.

19.
The Affair of Father Hugh Daly

I wish I could pass over the affair of Shelbyville's Father Hugh Daly. Our convent of Saint Mary of the Angels depended on his church for religious ministrations. I said "the affair,"--not a moral scandal, but a horrible scandalous proceeding.

It commenced in 1878 and lasted till 1890 when we left for Iowa. He accused us of attempted murder by poisoning at God's holy altar! How the public and newspapers seized on this story!

Father Daly, tall, with piercing eyes--he was a good pulpit orator. However, from his arrival at Shelbyville we noticed marked peculiarities along with his intellectual polish.

Sister Joseph had been serving as sacristan, taking care of the sacred utensils and vestments. Occasionally I assisted. One morning when I was alone, replacing the vestments after Mass, Father Daly rapidly strode into the sacristy, his eyes ablaze with fire.

"Are you in this damnable plot too, Sister Frances?" he bellowed.

I stared at him, speechless.

"Don't put on that innocent air," he said. "You're as guilty as the rest of them!"

"What do you mean, Father?" I managed to gasp.

"I mean that you are trying to get rid of me by slow murder. This morning I again found the poison. This time it was in the water served to me in Holy Mass!"

The vestment I was holding in my hands fell to the floor. I stood there dumbfounded.

"I want this matter solved right now," he bellowed as he waved his hands. "I'm going to expose the lot of you. Bring Sister Joseph over here immediately, and Mother Agnes too. I think they are the arch-conspirators in this plot to murder me."

I fled from his presence without daring to pick up the vestment from the floor. At the convent I rushed to Mother Agnes and stuttered out what had happened.

She whitened. "Either Father Daly is demented," she said, "or you are hallucinating, Sister Frances." She looked at me with a hard glance.

Mother Agnes sent for Sister Joseph and insisted that I accompany the two of them over to the church. We found Father Daly pacing the sacristy.

"Isn't this a pretty way you've fixed me?" he demanded. "What have I done to deserve this treatment?"

"Tell us, Father," said Mother Agnes, "just what is it you are driving at?"

"What you are driving at is my destruction!" he declared. "Sister Joseph here and the other Sisters have twice before administered poison to me in the wine served in holy Mass. This morning I again clearly detected it in the water."

Mother Agnes and Sister Joseph, horrified, protested their innocence. Mother Agnes and I, too, pleaded with him.

"I must know the kind of poison," he reiterated. "Unless you tell me, I'll denounce you to the people of this city and before tonight your convent will be burned to the ground!"

We appealed in the name of our dear Lord that he show reason.

"Enough now!" he said. "I'm going to have you arrested and hauled into court!"

"You have no evidence," said Mother Agnes.

"But I will have it," he rejoined. "The doctor will be here any minute. He'll prove I'm a poisoned man."

Father Daly took care, though, to send us home before the doctor arrived.

"What shall I do now?" wailed Mother Agnes. She was usually so imperturbable. Now, she wrung her hands. "What will the bishop think with this new trouble?"

Sister Jane de Chantal comforted Mother Agnes and suggested we bring no complaints. Silently leave the matter in the hands of God.

Father Daly's annoyance showed whenever he met us.

In two weeks Bishop McCloskey heard and took the next express from Louisville. He called at the Annunciation rectory.

When Father Daly came into the parlor he said, "Tis you, your lordship. How awful! You are in league with the Sisters in their plot to murder me."

Then, reproaching the bishop, Father Daly launched into a long litany of recriminations.

The Affair of Father Hugh Daly

At first Bishop McCloskey tried to reason, but Father Daly's voice roared louder. The neighbors surely heard.

The bishop hurried over to the convent. "Why didn't you tell me of this sooner?"

"Because of charity," answered Mother Agnes, "and the hope the matter would resolve itself quietly."

"The poor man is mad!" declared the bishop. "No doubt about that. This sick priest must be removed and put into an institution."

The bishop proceeded. The case was called up for the 25th of July and Father Daly was examined for lunacy in the court house at Shelbyville. However, without the proper collection of evidence, the lawyers and most of the doctors on the jury pronounced him sane.

As a consequence, the public suspected there was truth to Father Daly's accusations. Shelbyville, Louisville and Cincinnati newspapers carried long articles about the trial and Father Daly's vindication.

The Louisville *Courier-Journal* under the caption, "Father Daly's Strange Case," said:

"The article in regard to the Daly-McCloskey matter, which appeared in the *Courier-Journal* last Saturday, seems to have created considerable excitement in Louisville as well as in the entire country. To get at the other side of the story, your correspondent has interviewed C. M. Harwood, Esq. who assisted in the prosecution of Father Daly on the charge of insanity, with the following result:

"Mr. C. M. Harwood, Esquire: 'As this is a church matter you are asking me about, I desire to make the preliminary observation that I am not of blood kin to the Catholic church. I am only related by marriage.

"'I am descended from a Methodist stock for several generations back, but have sadly degenerated, until, in an orthodox sense, I am now an outcast in the religious world. Nat Robinson will tell you that my religious views should go to my credibility; and so let them.

"'As to the persecution of Father Daly by Bishop McCloskey, the truth is just the reverse. Father Daly is persecuting the Bishop, and the communication you call my attention to is an illustration of it. No intelligent person in this community, cognizant of the facts, has any doubt of the fact that Father Daly is the author of that article. It is true that the Bishop believed Father Daly to be insane, and that he caused an inquest to be held and it resulted in a verdict in

Daly's favor--But I am perfectly confident that the Bishop had nothing to do with any apparent haste in the matter. There is no doubt in my mind that Daly is slightly deranged. He is a monomaniac on the subject of being poisoned. There is a small society of nuns or Sisters near the Catholic church in this place. They are engaged in teaching a parochial school. They are as harmless and inoffensive set of ladies as could well be gathered together. Daly took up an idea they were trying to kill him with poison, and he entertained a great aversion to them and threatened to have their house burned down unless they would acknowledge they put poison in his altar wine. The Bishop could not convince him he was mistaken . . .

"'Several of the jury said to me after the trial was over they were satisfied Daly was not exactly of sound mind, but they did not think him insane to the extent that they would be justified in having him sent to an asylum at the expense of the State. I have not the slightest doubt that Bishop McCloskey sincerely believed Daly to be insane, and so believed it was his sacred duty to protect those defenseless and innocent nuns from his insane delusion.'"

The Sunday following the trial was the most ignominious day of humiliation and mortification that I ever lived through in my long life. The nuns were in their accustomed places in the front of the church at Mass when Father Daly delivered his sermon to the congregation. Clever preacher that he was, he pronounced what Sister Jane de Chantal called a "Phillipic of Vitriol," like Demosthenes's speeches against Phillip II of Spain--a declamation full of acrimonious invective. Daly abused the bishop, but he accused us Sisters of Saint Francis of almost every crime in the calendar. He said we were instrumental in having him arrested. By insinuation, we were guilty of attempted assassination.

He alluded in darkest terms to embarrassing episodes of our Order from the days of Aunt Caroline and Mother Angela to Mother Teresa.

When Bishop McCloskey learned of this sermon, he forbade us to receive the sacraments from Father Daly in the future.

But, we still had to sit in his church for Mass and listen to his tirades Sunday after Sunday. The people of Shelbyville, Catholics and Protestants, took sides. Some argued for Father Daly, others for the Sisters.

The Affair of Father Hugh Daly 91

Naturally, our school suffered. To shield our Order from public humiliation, the bishop then advised us to remain away from Mass. So, we had a kind of relief, but we were without Mass or the sacraments for weeks. Only occasionally a priest came from Louisville to hear our confessions and offer up the Sacrifice of the Mass in our Chapel. To me it seemed like the days of persecution in the old country.

Bishop McCloskey twice wrote Father Daly ordering him to leave Shelbyville, but Daly refused to yield. Instead, Father Daly started a petition among the people to have our Sisters removed and the Sisters of Charity substituted.

Our friends carried another petition for the removal of Father Daly. Clashes and fist-fights broke out between the two groups of petition-carriers. Newspapers spread the scandal.

In the summer of 1879, Father Daly retired to the home of a friend, threatening to appeal to Rome against the bishop and the Sisters. The bishop then appointed J. F. Reed as pastor for a time and we felt grand relief, attending the holy Mass and receiving the sacraments.

Two years of spiritual peace, and then we heard Father Daly had appealed his removal from Annunciation Parish all the way to Rome.

I don't know how things are done in Rome. I am a simple and, I trust, humble Franciscan nun, originally a girl from the Kentucky tobacco country. I realize that tremendous problems must be solved in Rome and that all things, under the Providence of God, work out for the best. Bishop McCloskey was not a churchman renowned for tact. His difficulties with pastors and his clash with Father Abbot Benedict of Gethsemane had not been forgotten in Rome. Father Daly found support in Father Devied and Father Chambige who were in Rome with former cases against Bishop McCloskey.

The result? Bishop McCloskey was ordered to reinstate Father Daly. In October of 1881, the angry priest returned triumphant to Shelbyville to resume charge of the Annunciation parish. He gave the Sisters trouble two more years.

Then one day, Bishop McCloskey arrived for a profession at the convent. "You have suffered long enough, dear Sisters," he announced kindly. "You haven't complained, but I have heard of your difficulties. I have good news for you."

We sat erect and expectant in our chapel.

"It is true that you are a small community, but I am going to give you your own chaplain for your convent."

One could almost hear the sigh of relief from all of us.

"I am going to send you an aged priest, but one whom you all know and love, Father Eliseus Durbin."

Mother Agnes arose and, bowing first to the altar, she addressed the bishop: "May God requite your lordship for this favor. We rejoice at this news. And we promise to make dear Father Durbin a grand welcome."

So it was that venerable Father Durbin came to live in the house next to our convent. He cheered us and we all exulted in the Lord. Now we Sisters could hear Mass daily in our own chapel, and were free from Father Daly's taunts.

Father Durbin served us faithfully without salary up to the time of his death in March, 1887. Almost ninety when he died, he had been one of the heroic missioners on horseback in the pioneer days of Kentucky. He died penniless, but our little community out of its own poverty paid his funeral expenses and even erected a suitable monument over his grave in Saint Louis cemetery in Louisville.

20.
Christian Tact

After the Chicago Hill schism, anxiety thicker than ever settled on our community in Shelbyville. The severe deprivations didn't help.

Mother Agnes wrote to the bishop:

> "Our Lady of the Angels
> "Shelbyville
> "July 2, 1880

"Right Reverend Bishop McCloskey
"My dear Father:

"Necessity compels me to write and give you a clear statement of our financial condition. Yesterday I sent the last ten dollars I had to pay a bill for coffee. The account at the mill is again nearly in the hundreds, the grocery bill is about $50, the last three loads of coal are unpaid for. Everything in the house in the way of groceries is now exhausted. Some old bills still to be settled and the house itself in a sad state of repair. All these things to meet and not a cent in the world with which to do it. Day by day I see (without being able to avert it) the slow but sure decline of the Sisters' health and strength, and all for the want of substantial food and nourishment. Now while it is cheap, we should store in our winter's coal, but we cannot think of that, much less do it.

"The support derived from our school is scarcely worth its name. We have considered and reconsidered this matter, and we are forced to admit that under present circumstances we can see no hope, neither present nor future, for our struggling community, unless immediate steps are taken to insure our support. All this--added to the unpleasant state of affairs here, makes it for us, a thing almost insupportable. Right Reverend Father, as long as I had or expected to have a dollar I struggled along and refrained from worrying you about our poverty, but now we are compelled to inform you, as we, of ourselves, can do nothing, but with your good advice something could be done. We are most willing to work day and night to help ourselves if we but get the work and a good place in which to do it.

"Anxiously awaiting your reply, I remain, dear Father,
Your sincere child in Christ,
Sister Mary Agnes."

Mother Agnes wrote again in 1881:

"Matters are even more depressing than when I last wrote to you.

"The bill for meal was handed to me yesterday amounting to $108. A notice from Benz Bros. was sent to me a few weeks ago stating that he would send his draft for $56; part of this amount has been due since 1875. Today I received the enclosed notice to have the front paving repaired; this will cost at least twenty or thirty dollars. We have neither meat, potatoes nor coal for the winter and the convent itself is going to ruin for the want of repairs.

"We can expect no assistance from the people here. The affair of Father Hugh Daly is ever before them. Further, when asked why they do not help us, they reply, 'Let them go out and work as we do.' Then the clergymen of the Diocese, as a body--ever since our departure from Mount Olivet--are opposed to us and desire nothing more than to see us dispensed. It is certainly unjust to condemn us for the conduct of those who are no longer here. And it is hard to meet with such treatment from those whom we would expect to be a help to the weak and a consolation to the afflicted."

Bishop McCloskey helped as he could, but there were frequent limits to his generosity. And it wasn't financial aid we were looking for--we wanted schools. As a teaching Order we could use our talents and make our own decent living by working for the glory of God and for His children. The bishop had promised us one or two good schools in Louisville, but we had a personality conflict and now the bishop procrastinated.

We simply must reopen our abandoned academy of Saint Clare's at Chicago Hill, install some of our best sisters there, and fight for our survival.

But, on the Chicago, Kentucky, scene stood Father Edmund Drury--a zealous priest, and a good one according to his lights, but a bitter and dangerous enemy of our embattled little Order. His hostility sprang from Mother Angela's and Bishop McCloskey's treatment of Father Abbot Benedict while we were at Olivet.

Drury had been what we called "the evil genius" behind the revolt of the nuns at Saint Clare's. He had wanted our Sisters at Saint Clare's to join the Sisters of Loretto. But the Loretto community wouldn't take them without the Saint Clare property. We wouldn't relinquish our land claims and we had successfully resisted Father Drury.

Father Drury passionately opposed our re-establishment at Chicago Hill. Four years he opposed us, sometimes quietly, sometimes flaring out violently. When Mother Agnes went to Chicago Hill to reopen Saint Clare's, she so dreaded Father Drury she took the county sheriff along to protect her. Father Drury burned with fury and never forgot it.

We sent the gifted Sister Magdalen Mattingly with four other nuns to reopen Chicago Hill. Only nine pupils returned to the school at first, but as the numbers increased Drury's opposition increased. He had a lot of influence in the community and he held meetings of protest. He dared not openly defy the bishop who had sent our Sisters. But among Drury's supporters was Father Viola of the neighboring parish who could. At these meetings Father Viola would say, "You Franciscans should give up your claims to the school and property."

Then Father Drury would rise and declare passionately: "The rights of our congregations must be protected!"

However, our number of pupils grew and several talented young women from Louisville noticed our stand and came to be admitted.

Of course, Father Drury was indignant and vexed about this. But, fearless man that he was, he wrote Mother Agnes that he was coming to Our Lady of the Angels at Shelbyville to thresh out the matter with us. Mother asked Sister Jane de Chantal and me to be with her when he arrived. We received him in a friendly manner and after the usual amenities he opened the attack.

"It has become my duty," he said, "to advise some postulants who wish to embrace the holy rule of Saint Francis. So, I have to come to you for information."

"We are glad you did, Father," answered Mother. "We'll help if we can."

Father began his series of taunts: "Well, you know, Sisters, the reports about the trial of Father Daly."

"Naturally," replied Mother. "What about them?"

"Why, Sisters, time and again he has publicly charged you with being the cause of his troubles."

"Indeed, he has," said Mother. "And he's made the same accusations against the bishop. Do you believe these charges?"

Father Drury flushed and said angrily: "Whether I do or not is beside the question. This I do know, however, and you can't deny it: The Sisters here never go to Mass--not even on Sundays!"

"That's often true, dear Father," said Mother Agnes gently, "but his lordship, your own bishop, has ordered it that way for the time being."

"But Mother," he continued, "they don't go to confession and communion except when some priest comes from a distance to give them an opportunity. This is a strange state of things. Don't you see? Your pastor at your door and the church within a stone's throw, and still, no Mass, no sacraments, except when a priest comes from the city or elsewhere."

When Mother Agnes remained silent, Sister Jane de Chantal spoke softly: "Father, you know very well the reasons behind all this and so it isn't necessary for Mother to explain them to you."

"Possibly I do," he said, "but it is doubly painful for me to hear these things since I have your Sisters at Saint Clare's in Chicago Hill. Furthermore, now it's my duty to advise those ladies about entering the community. They either don't know these reports or they don't believe them. I need to know the truth. I can't send those young people to a place where they don't have Mass on Sundays. Nor would I be treating your community with due consideration if I tried to discourage them."

"Due consideration?" I interjected. "When did you show consideration to our community?" May God forgive me. I know it wasn't my place to speak, but I felt it so deeply and I believe Mother and Sister Jane did too.

Then Father stormed: "If this community isn't in a condition to train novices in the practice of virtue, I'm obliged to advise young women against entering."

But our visit ended on an outwardly friendly tone before Father Drury left.

And I will add here that applications from Chicago and that vicinity continued through the years and we were very happy to accept a number of young ladies who were endowed with true vocations.

Christian Tact

The head-on opposition of Father Drury and his supporters continued and, if anything, increased in ferocity. The number of students increased, but often due to Father Drury's influence with their parents, pupils were withdrawn.

And there were humiliating events for the Sisters. For instance, the coal for heating our buildings was owned communally by the Sisters' school and by Father Drury's parish. Due to the inability of the Sisters to pay their share one winter, the two trustees of the parish ordered a team of horses and wagon to haul away our half of the coal. And the thermometer was below zero that day.

"I actually had to steal and hide enough fuel to burn until we could get more," Sister Aloysius recalled years later. (She had succeeded Sister Magdalen as superior.)

"Stealing under those circumstances was rather a virtue than a vice," I assured her.

But the coal was actually all hauled away right under the Sister's eyes. One of the elegant gentleman, a parish trustee who was present and a witnesss to this act, remarked in the Sisters' presence, "If we can't get them out of Saint Clare's any other way, we will freeze them out."

As a result, when Bishop McCloskey came to give the sacrament of Confirmation not long after this, he seized the occasion to denounce the extremists who had opposed our community, and to embarrass Father Drury with his remarks. Affairs began to improve at Chicago Hill after this--slowly at first, but surely. Our school attendance later soared to a record height and our Sisters had a wonderful music class at the academy. One half of the class consisted of the children of the leading Protestant citizens of the town.

God's grace wrought a new wonder. Father Edmund Drury was won over by the Christian tact and bravery of our nuns, became an admirer of our Order and was a loyal friend through the following years. In fact I met him at various times in later life and he even made a friendly visit to us in Iowa.

21.
Begging

We hoped and prayed for a good school in Louisville. We needed the income for our starving community. But, we were forever disappointed. Anxious to labor anywhere, our eager Sisters took missions far from our convent in Shelbyville.

The first mission was in far-off western Kentucky, at tiny Knottsville, near Owensboro. At the invitation of Father Rock four of our Sisters opened Saint Lawrence's School, November, 1881, a pleasant and successful mission. The school started with seventy-eight pupils and with Father Rock's loyal co-operation, we increased to one hundred and twenty by the end of the year.

We opened Saint Jerome's School with fifteen pupils at Fancy Farm in 1882. We soon grew to fifty pupils. In the lovely region of extreme Western Kentucky, where the Ohio joins the Mississippi, Fancy Farm was founded by a colony of Maryland Catholics, descendants of Lord Baltimore's brave English immigrants. The main difference between them and my people of Marion County was that they had been Northern sympathizers during the Civil War.

In October of 1884 Father King invited us to open Saint Mary's School at Whitesville ten miles south of Knottsville. We started there with fifty pupils.

All three of those mission schools were small, struggling, pioneer ventures of Catholicity in Western Kentucky. Our poor Order put everything we had into them. We didn't reap a great material reward, but our spiritual benefits were remarkable, especially in regard to the number of gracious young women of old Kentucky families who came in as postulants.

During these years we even received an appeal from a missionary priest in the Colorado Rockies. We had to refuse him.

Then, in 1884, an offer came from the Franciscan Father Provincial, Father Lucan Godttbehoede, of Saint Patrick's

School in Minonk, Illinois. This was the most promising, flattering offer ever made to us--for convent and quarters, for school and income and for a secure future. All our friends pressed us to accept it. Even Father Abbot Benedict heard of it and advised us to move our entire colony of nuns from Kentucky to Minonk. Mother Agnes was for it and so was her council. I was for it and so was the community. But, here again, Bishop McCloskey intervened, frowned darkly on the project and refused his permission. I've often wondered what Providence might have had in store for us if we had moved to Illinois. But seeing how God has blessed us now in Iowa I am thankful for the bishop's preemptory refusal.

Our mission schools didn't lighten our economic burden. We lived by "doing without." More novices took the places of Sisters in the field so we had the support of them. "Pauper's diet," Sister Dolorosa said. "That's why so many of us are sick; we aren't eating, and what we have is the same coarse and monotonous fare."

In addition, some of the Sisters were now growing old and feeble and we had their care.

Mother Agnes wrote again for help:

"Convent of Our Lady
Shelbyville, Ky.
Jan. 20, 1885

"Right Reverend dear Father:

"I regret having to trouble you again by a repetition of our difficulties occasioned by our extreme poverty.

"I have been for the last two months, and especially since the New Year set in, besieged by our creditors who will wait no longer for settlement. I see no recourse but to be sold out for debt if something is not done to relieve us. The schools we have are so poor they do not support the Sisters who are teaching them, much less help the Mother House.

"The sufferings here are heartrending to witness and endure. Sisters, whether well or ill, fare the same. I can't look on in silence. There's no hope . . . present or future--for the preservation of our community.

"This continual struggle with poverty along with other and more bitter trials has shattered my health and almost driven me to distraction.

"Your Lordship's troubled child,
Sister M. Agnes, Superior."

Begging

Shortly after this date came a joyful little incident that brought us some temporary relief. What should come up the street one morning and pull to a halt in front of our convent, but a well-loaded wagon drawn by a pair of mules and driven by my old black friend, Andrew Jackson Pendleton!

I don't imagine Andrew Jackson ever received a warmer welcome in his life than that morning when our Sisters clustered about his wagon. I almost hugged the kind, old man as he stood there with his cap in his hand looking inquiringly about for me.

Pa had sent Andrew Jackson up from his Saint Mary's plantation in Marion County with a load of every variety of vegetables and fruits he could lay his hands on. With the load came a note from Pa, chiding me for not having informed him earlier of the poverty we were suffering. "You need not pretend a brave front before your Pa," my father wrote. "I shall send more goods to you in the future."

We warmed up Andrew Jackson with hot coffee and lunch before he left in the afternoon. I knew that his dear Patience had died about the time that Ma had. I asked Jackson if he remembered his wife's soul in his prayers.

"Yes, indeed, Miss Sally." He never addressed me as anything but Miss Sally.

I wished him Godspeed and sent my fondest love to Pa.

In spite of his help, however, and really as a result of our community's long and continuous torment, we were compelled to resort to what many people considered a shameful thing. We resorted to begging--begging on a grand scale. We referred to it euphemistically as "collecting for the convent."

Right up to 1890 when we left for Iowa there were begging excursions every year. Two Sisters would carry out the task, usually for two weeks, occasionally longer, once for two months. At first we visited the cities and towns of our diocese only and always with the approval of the Bishop McCloskey who saw no other alternative for our existence and survival.

Mother Agnes wished to write to Archbishop Pechan for permission to beg in the great city of Chicago, but his lordship forbade that. She did gain the permission, however, of Archbishop Elder for our excursion through Cincinnati, but Bishop McCloskey was quite furious when he first heard about it and soon upbraided her. But her apologies and tears won him over for Cincinnati and also for Indiana.

Some begging ventures brought in only forty dollars, several netted us two hundred dollars, and the two Sisters who returned from the long excursion of over two months brought with them almost a thousand dollars in cash, food, clothing and religious supplies such as a handsome statue of Saint Francis and some beautiful adornments for our chapel.

I was asked to go on one of these trips, but I never went again. I so wanted to be humble, but I could not swallow my pride. I was thoroughly ashamed. The petty humiliations, the cold disdain, the contemptuous refusals in homes or in businesses embarrassed me horribly and Mother yielded to my pleadings never to be sent out again. Sister Jane de Chantal, who had engaged in more than one successful expedition, agreed with me that I was not the type for such work.

"You make a far better school teacher," she comforted me, and then she informed me that the bishop had just sent us a bank draft for a hundred and fifty dollars.

"I happen to know how he obtained that particular money," Sister Dolorosa told us, with a slightly superior smile.

"How?" we asked her.

"I'm not absolutely certain of the story," she said. "But I do know that he sold his carriage and team. And I was told that he had received a hundred and fifty dollars for the horses, so I think I'm correct in supposing that that's where our money came from."

"It's noble of him to turn over that money to us, and extremely charitable, no doubt," said Sister Magdalen, a usually gentle and always wise nun. "But with just reason, he is feeling more and more responsible for the temporal welfare of our community."

"With just reason?" asked Sister Jane. "Do you, too, think he has twinges of conscience?"

"Indeed, yes," said Sister Magdalen. "The poor man frankly admits it more by his actions than by his words. He feels remorse for having been so very persistent in urging the community to remove the Mother House from Mount Olivet. There, at least, we never suffered without basics of food and clothing."

Such was our dejection, that this long submerged thought about Mount Olivet would occasionally rankle and come to the surface even amongst our holiest nuns.

Abbot Benedict wrote us from Gethsemane about the widespread criticisms he had heard of our policy of begging and pleaded with Mother Agnes to desist from the practice. She wrote him in reply: "Our Holy Father, Saint Francis, and his companions begged alms from door to door. If it was not wrong for them to do so, it certainly is not for us, his poor children."

In the fall of 1884 while Mother Agnes and Sister Josephine were collecting in Indiana they paid a visit to the Oldenburgh Franciscan convent, the parent house of our community. Reverend Mother Olivia received them cordially and when they left for home gave them a liberal donation of material for winter clothing. But a far more important result of that visit was the strict reintroduction of the Rule of Saint Francis in our distracted community. During those years we had been shunned by some of the clergy as a strange order and even the members of other religious communities looked upon us as a sort of spiritual pariah or low caste.

Lacking the many helpful outside religious contacts that we should have had and guided only periodically by the pious priests who were our retreat masters, our enforcedly inbred spiritual program was probably not as progressively Franciscan as it should have been.

Mother Agnes obtained a German copy of the full Rule from Mother Olivia and had it translated into English by Father Ubaldus of the Franciscan Monastery in Louisville. Through the help of the Franciscan fathers there, the full richness, beauty and discipline of the Rule soon flourished at home and in our missions.

During this span of years as well as for years to come, Mother Agnes was chosen as superior at every triennial election and usually by a unanimous vote. At this period she seemed, to us at least, an inspired leader. She held us loyally together in the face of every threatening difficulty and aided us both by wise counsel and courageous action.

22.
Brides of Christ

It has always seemed to me that God must have loved our little Order dearly or the storms that swirled about our Franciscan ark would have sunk us. I've thought it was a mark of God's purpose that young women continued to apply. Our poverty didn't frighten them away. Why should our struggling, starving and despised group of dedicated women have drawn so many generous young souls--especially from Kentucky where our status was well known?

Our chapel seats were never empty long. Postulants begged to be admitted though we suffered losses from death brought on by malnutrition. Postulants left at the end of probation. Others wisely returned home before pronouncing longer vows. Two or three committed grave disobedience and were dismissed. Still this was a small number in light of the hardships. And the applications for vocations overwhelmed us.

Two Miss Hancocks and their cousin, Miss Van Wie, came from New York with a letter from their pastor. Why had they chosen our little community? Typical New York society girls, bubbling with gaiety and nervous in their intentions, they brought half a dozen trunks filled with silks and laces, the finest chinaware and silverware. They had handsome colored sunshades, fans and parasols. One had a badminton set hidden. All had crystal and pearl rosaries and lovely morocco-bound prayer-books.

Mother Agnes received them doubtfully. They were pious. We loved them and laughed at their antics. The shock of our poverty was too much, though they bravely held out for two months. When they left we wept and laughed with them at parting. They delved into their trunks and insisted we accept gifts. Most of them were such a luxury we could never use them. When their carriage drove to the railway station with the three gaily waving their handkerchiefs, we felt sad for awhile.

Also, from 1883 through 1885 we received some of the grandest vocations! From the old Maryland Catholic families near our Fancy Farm mission in the far western corner of Kentucky came Carricos, the Willits, the Piercalls, the Roberts and others. But there are five of them I must mention in particular because all have been with me the years since. They have become pillars of our Franciscan Order--superiors and directors of novices and famous teachers and courageous examples of holiness--Allie Higdon from Owensboro, later Sister Mary Lawrence; three from Fancy Farm: Laura Carrico, illustrious Mother Paul of the Cross; Victoria Curtsinger who at thirty-eight became Sister Mary Columba and Lula Ryan who was eighteen when she became Sister Mary Xavier. Finally came Rose Schneider of the artists' family of Schneiders in Louisville. She was the niece of the internationally famous organist Frederick Schneider and friend of the family of Johann Sebastian Bach. Then, there was Rose, later Sister Mary Carmel, who would head the music department of Mount Saint Clare College in Clinton.

Brides of Christ with me for a long time on this earth--how long will it be till we meet with Him above?

23.
Yearning for Olivet

That name of Mount Olivet! What nostalgic, what hypnotic memories that name always awakened in us in those days! Ever since the unfortunate hour of our departure, we older Sisters, Sister Jane and Mother Agnes--innocent victims--sighed and prayed for the repossession of our old home. We yearned to be there to carry on our intended work.

In September of 1884, Father Edmund Drury of Chicago Hill, once our enemy, now our friend, invited Mother Agnes to join his pilgrimage to the Grotto of Lourdes on the grounds of Gethsemane Abbey. He was leading the Sisters and students of Saint Clare's academy there on the feast of Saint Francis, October 4th.

Mother joyfully accepted. She was anxious to meet Father Abbot Benedict and see Mount Olivet if possible. So, she asked Sister Jane and me to accompany her.

For the two of us, it was a means of recapturing a past ecstasy. We "pilgrims" arrived for the high Mass celebrated by the Right Reverend Abbot himself. Afterward he received us all but failed to recognize Mother Agnes. She had only been at Mount Olivet a few weeks before her mother had called her home. He laughed heartily and seized our hands. He led us aside for a little chat. The grand old man's hair was nearly white, but his actions were vigorous and his eyes as bright and steely as ever.

"You are all invited to dinner," he called to the group. "After dinner I'm taking Father Drury and these three Sisters in our carriage over to see Mount Olivet."

What a wonderful sight it was when we later reached the spot and gazed upon the Mount!

"Why, it is more beautiful than ever," Sister Jane gasped. "What have you been doing to it, Father Abbot?"

"Oh, I must explain," he said. "I've had the grounds and buildings touched up. This summer I offered Mount Olivet to the Josephite Fathers to establish an orphan asylum for black children. Father Benoit, the rector of Mill Hill

College, near London, came to see the place. It was to impress him I had it touched up. He was enthusiastic."

"You mean," asked Mother Agnes, "he's taking it over?"

"Unfortunately, no," said Father Abbot. "When he spoke to Bishop McCloskey about it and proposed bringing his Sisters from England, the bishop refused to receive those Sisters." He glanced at Mother Agnes. "The bishop made one remark about your community working here again. It was a vague remark, and then he dropped the subject."

"He did?" asked Mother Agnes. She didn't pursue the question, but her eyes showed a new light. I could almost read her daring thoughts.

The pastoral scene, the panorama before us, had a profound sentimental effect on us. There in all its loveliness stood the stately main building with its white walls, red roof and still-green vine-covered verandas. I could hear in my memory the songs of children again and the music of their laughter.

Though Olivet was remote from town or railroad, its peaceful beauty made it an Eden, a suitable spot for praise and meditation. Surrounded by high hills, called knobs, the graceful evergreen cover of trees made the setting picturesque. Not a house in sight, the convent seemed set in a wilderness, an ideal place for a secluded life. Across this chosen spot where nature had lavished such care, we saw Negroes working in the fields with their mules. The women's varicolored "Mother Hubbards" and sun bonnets glistened in the afternoon sun. The soft sounds of a spiritual they were crooning carried across to us. As I looked at Sister Jane, I saw tears slipping down her cheeks.

24.
Back to Olivet?

We began the battle for the recapture of Mount Olivet, at first spasmodically and then continuously. The remark made by Abbot Benedict to Mother Agnes became the spark to set her zeal afire. The thought of Abbot turning over "our" haven to some other Order made Mother Agnes' eyes blaze. And Mother's determination was the fiercest I ever saw. The lamp of Shelbyville's flame burned low and our missions flickered on a low wick. By returning to Mount Olivet we could escape from debt and misery.

Abbot Benedict sent us this declaration drawn by our venerable benefactor, Mr. Ben F. Mattingly, legally recorded October 21st, 1884:

"When the Right Reverend Abbot of Gethsemane, Dom Benedict established in 1866, with the consent of the Right Reverend Lavialle, Bishop of Louisville, a school for poor girls at Mount Olivet, Nelson County, Kentucky, about one mile from his Abbey, I helped him to carry on his plans and to put the new institution on good footing. I considered that it is a good and holy thing to educate poor little girls who are without parents and friends and to teach them how to love God and become useful members of society and good Christians. I saw the Institution productive of good during several years and I regret very much to have witnessed its fall. But the Abbot of Gethsemane could not prevent its destruction and now I declare that I leave into his hands and into the hands of his successors the whole of the money (about 10,000 dollars) I spent to clear Mount Olivet from debts and secure its success.

"The farm being now the legal property of the Abbey, which administers it, I hope that at some future time, the Abbey will be able to reopen the school, or to establish in its place an orphan asylum for colored children who have no home in the Diocese, or to use it for some other like charitable purposes, at his discretion, for instance for the support of a male school attached to the Abbey for the benefit of the poor.

"I am willing also for him to sell the farm and to give the money to the Little Sisters of the Poor.

"Meanwhile I wish him to continue to use the revenue to have some poor girls instructed at the Sisters' School of New Haven and elsewhere. As far as I can judge I am fully convinced that other benefactors who helped the Abbot, unanimously concur with my views, and would not withdraw from his hands what they entrusted to his care."

A voluminous correspondence began between Mother Agnes and the abbot on the one hand, and Mother and the bishop on the other for the purpose of bringing about the return of at least some of our Sisters to the Mount.

The abbot, because of his past sorry experience, insisted on preliminary discussions and legal safeguards. The bishop, cautious, hesitant and slow, breathing sometimes hot and sometimes cold, never gave an outright refusal. Our hopes were kept alive.

Mother encountered the abbot one day visiting the Sisters at Saint Clare's, Chicago Hill. The two tried to thresh out the difficulties. The abbot finally said, "Mother, you must prepare a complete plan--for support, for a chaplain, for repairs, for everything--so that my community can see it."

"I assure you," she said, "that we can and will do everything within the bounds of reason."

"Well and good," said the abbot, "but I am determined not to be fooled again. My lawyer, Governor William Johnson, will arrange my business."

"That's agreeable to me," replied Mother Agnes. "You take Governor Johnson for your lawyer. I will take Saint Joseph for mine and leave it to him to arrange all for the glory of God and the good of both parties."

And so the discussions continued to drag on.

Then Sister Jane de Chantal took sick and died after two weeks, August 3, 1885--a tragedy, felt by the entire community, but more sharply by me. I was with her, praying constantly. She was my dearest friend and my spiritual model as well as the staunch pillar of our poor little congregation. Only fifty-two years of age, this lovely belle of New Orleans, Elizabeth Batre, had become the greatest saint I knew on earth. The grand consolation for her was that she had again seen Mount Olivet at its fairest. The year before she died she had seen that hallowed home where as novice, professed Sister and Mother Superior she spent the happiest and most peaceful years of her life.

Back to Olivet? 111

Now and for the next two years Bishop McCloskey constantly advised the sale of our Shelbyville property to pay off our mounting debts. We were anxious to sell, if we could find a location for our mother house, and, especially, if we could return to Mount Olivet. We had hopes for awhile of selling it to the Sisters of Charity for $10,000.00. Even the Baptists had looked at it with the idea of starting a small seminary in Shelbyville.

The bishop also urged us to move to Knottsville where we had a mission school. Father Gambou was appointed spiritual director of our Order and made pastor of Knottsville so he could prepare us to move our novitiate and mother house. But as months rolled on, plans failed. An army of creditors worried us. Destitution seemed our destiny.

At last the bishop stopped pushing Knottsville--too far from railroad or steam boat. The Knottsville people weren't committed to education enough to take their children from picking worms in the tobacco fields. Father Gambou balked at moving the mother house.

Meanwhile, Abbot Benedict agreed to receive us at Mount Olivet on certain conditions. Along with other concessions, we had to promise never to establish an academy along with our school for poor children, never to introduce a music course, and never to go out begging![25] On his part, he would find us means of support. Mother Agnes, therefore, traveled to Louisville and dramatically addressed his lordship. "Dear Father," she said, "the day is at hand when God is about to (place) in our possession a home fixed permanently on unshaken ground and in His holy Name, Right Reverend Bishop, I beseech you on bended knees at your feet to grant me your blessing and consent to negotiate with Father Abbot."[26]

The bishop granted her plea, but, only for a few Sisters to open a school for poor girls at Mount Olivet and not for the return of the community to it as their home.

What had actually wrung this concession from McCloskey was a threat. Mother Agnes had written:

"If this present petition is not granted, we ask to be permitted to seek a home in another diocese for our struggling and half-starved community. Our few branch houses are not much better off than ourselves and consequently cannot assist us in the least. There is now a means open to insure us, not only honest and honorable bread, but also a permanent home. To reject that proffered means, under such favorable terms as are stipulated by Father Abbot, would be to write our own death sentence as a community here."

And so, at last, on August 19th, 1887, in the abbey dining room at Gethsemane, Father Abbot and Mother Agnes put their signatures to a document conveying to us the industrial school. Thus ended the long struggle between the bishop, the abbot and the Sisters for the reopening of Mount Olivet Primary School for Girls. "Praise God!" said both Abbot Benedict and Mother Agnes.

As I was the only surviving founder of our Order--the only surviving nun of the original group at Mount Olivet and before that at Calvary Hill--I was asked to be among the five to re-establish the home.

We arrived by train at Gethsemane on the 25th of August and the little wooden wagon took us to the abbey. All the abbey bells had been ordered to be rung in our honor. Father Abbot met us as we descended, welcomed us and gave us his blessing. We were then driven over to the Mount.

On entering the house and taking possession in the holy name of God, we knelt and quietly offered prayer, imploring Heaven's blessing upon the place and ourselves.

The next weeks we put buildings into repair. We went after furniture and wiped up fourteen years of accumulated dust.

Every morning at five we started the mile on foot to the abbey over the rough stones of the wagon road to hear holy Mass.

In two weeks we had things humming, despite privations. On September 7th we started with ten pupils. This soon increased to fifteen day scholars and eight work scholars.

At my suggestion, we arranged a formal opening of our re-established institution and we set the celebration for the feast of Saint Francis, October 4th. We sent invitations to the bishop and a list of clergymen. Not one even responded, except for Father Joseph O'Grady, who'd been our confessor at Shelbyville. We thanked him for offering holy Mass--the first time for us in the chapel in fourteen years.

Abbot Benedict showed his kindness by giving us three hundred dollars in cash, three healthy cows, three weaned calves, and eighteen head of his best sheep. He donated vestments, altar articles, chalice and ciborium, wire and pickets for fencing, a supply of lumber and nails, and he paid the bill for the painting of the upper story of our building.

The Franciscan fathers of Louisville also sent us vestments, a carved missal stand and a beautiful ostensorium for displaying the Host. One of our neighbors, Captain Harris, gave us a horse and another neighbor, Mrs. Morrison, gave us a mule.

Inspired by this success, Mother Agnes made further efforts to place our Sisters in new missions. She hoped to stop the further swing of the ill-fortune pendulum. We opened school in Herdinsburg. By invitation Sister Magdalen and four Sisters opened a larger one, at Saint Charles in Marion County, near my home. In 1812 at Saint Charles the famous Kentucky missionary, Father Charles Nerincks, had started the Loretto Sisterhood--the Friends of Mary at the Foot of the Cross--in a log house.

We opened a one-room free school for black children. About the same time we commenced a larger free school for the black children of Chicago Hill.

After we had been at Olivet a year or two, Pa died. My brother drove me back in his carriage from Marion County where we had remained for a few days to attend to Pa's funeral. That grand old man, Hugh Walker, had lived to be eighty and had survived Ma by almost ten years.

I had the sad happiness to be with Pa before he died. We hadn't seen each other for years since his long illness had kept him home. He had continued to send me encouraging and inspiring letters. When I entered his sick room, he smiled and said aloud: "Now dismiss Thy servant, O Lord!" That pious old Kentuckian! How I loved him!

At the internment service in the graveyard, I wept as I had never wept before, and I was not ashamed. I felt that a world of goodness had left me then, but he had built in enough dykes to help me withstand the floods.

Back at school the girls met me on the lawn. We had over forty students now. They escorted me to the hall, all assuring me that they had prayed for Pa's soul. The Sisters met me with their kind condolences on the porch as we sat down for a few minutes.

"I wish," said Sister Dolorosa, "that we had better news to sweeten your return. But, you might as well hear our distress."

"We should be used to distress by now, shouldn't we?" I asked.

"First of all," she said, "the bishop has taken away our chaplain again."

We hadn't had the last one very long.

"So its the old story," I said, "marching the children in the early mornings down the long, rough road." The road to the parish church by the abbey was not made for little feet. How many times we'd walked the ruts and the rocks, the children sniffling in the cold.

"Then," said Sister Rose,[27] "the bishop wrote a strict letter that no Sister is to go to the Abbey of Gethsemane under any pretext. If any Sister breaks this rule, she will not get absolution except from him. He made it a 'reserved case.' The next day he softened it by saying, we shouldn't go to the abbey every day. You know yourself, Sister Frances, that we haven't been there for two months. You were there with me on that last visit."

I well recalled that last visit to Abbot Benedict. We had teased the old gentleman about letting us have music courses in our school. He laughingly refused and again condemned such subjects as "modern foolishness for poor girls." Then we had become serious and brought up the matter of an academy or high school. That was our old argument for Mount Olivet.

"I've told you time and again," he explained, "your school is only for poor girls. Academies are for the rich."

"But dear Father Abbot," we objected, "we are growing. We've expanded enough to teach both elementary and secondary."

"No, no," he countered. "You are a teaching Order who must stay with simple, practical teaching. Let other Sisters teach the rich in their academies."

Then he added more sternly, raising his voice, "No music! No academies! I pray to God to send fire from heaven and burn Mount Olivet when anyone establishes an academy there!"

That was the tone of our last visit. Now I could sense the Sisters' alarm at this new, severe attitude of the bishop.

"The news from Our Lady of the Angels at Shelbyville is much worse," Sister Rose continued. She seemed relieved to be able to pour out her laments. "Bishop McCloskey, so generous for awhile, has now closed his hand toward us. He has refused from now on to pay our loan's interest. He said he'd paid in the past as part of his duty. No more. We simply don't know where to raise the money."

"Why, I thought some of our Sisters were out on a collecting expedition right now," I said.

"Little good that does," said Sister Rose. "The bishop has forbidden Mother Agnes to go to other dioceses where we might really get help. Mother said if the Church permitted the starving to steal bread it should allow us Sisters to seek help."

"With God's grace," said Sister Dolorosa, "our heads are still above water. The lectures, entertainments and bazaar we sponsored in Louisville and Shelbyville helped."

But Sister Rose saw the dark side, a predicament worse than I suspected. "We can be without a chaplain," she said, "but the Sisters in Shelbyville have no chaplain and are now commanded by the bishop to go to Father Daly."

"A few of them did go," said Sister Michael.

"And never dared go again," added Sister Rose. "For ten weeks they had no confessor. The Blessed Sacrament wasn't changed in their chapel for all that time. Then the bishop ordered it removed. Now, without their last spiritual consolation, the Sisters are grieving."

"Tell what Mother proposes," said Sister Dolorosa.

Sister Rose turned to me. "We are praying the nine first Fridays that the Father Daly problem will be solved at Shelbyville. We know the Sacred Heart will grant that request."

"I'll do it," I answered. "With every postulant, novice and professed Sister joining in I'm sure our prayers will be granted."

"Speaking of postulants," said Sister Rose, "his lordship claims we can't support the members we have now and wants Mother Agnes to refuse future candidates."

"Well," I asked, "hasn't the bishop justification?"

"No!" said Sister Rose. "Mother Agnes said, 'No more risk now than for the past fifteen years. We have choice novices begging to be received. It's an injustice to refuse them their happiness. The life of our community depends on their admission.'"

I didn't say anything. I was uneasy. What was the future? Why had Bishop McCloskey turned against us? He had been our only friend. Was he angry over the few of us who returned to Mount Olivet?

Each month brought misfortune. The school at Knottsville closed. The Sisters' salaries hadn't been paid for two years. The school at Whitesville ran hundreds of dollars in debt and we failed at a settlement. Our academy at Shelbyville, poor and spurned by Father Daly, realized only seven dollars a month. We supported our entire community from the three hundred dollars we took in from parochial schools tuition, from Mount Olivet and from begging.

In spite of this, our debt increased only a thousand dollars a year. It would have been more, but we did without many essentials.

One year we received not a dollar from the parish or school of Fancy Farm--and how it was neglected, spiritually. The Sisters were without a resident priest and without Mass, confession and Communion except twice a month. Food was a problem. One of the Sisters wrote that young Carlos, the Saint Bernard puppy adopted by the Sisters, was "growing so fast that it was a problem to find food and bones for him."

When Bishop McCloskey remained adamant, Mother Agnes and Sister Magdalen went to see the Archbishop of Cincinnati. They told him our story and begged counsel. Archbishop Elder told Mother Agnes, "You lay out your case to Bishop McCloskey once more, wait a reasonable time and then return to him. If he doesn't act, I will."

Then occurred a strange answer to prayer. Father Hugh Daly left Shelbyville. Neither the Sisters nor the congregation had Mass the following Sunday. What sincere thanks we offered up when the new pastor arrived!

Months later, October 4th, 1889, Bishop McCloskey called at Our Lady of the Angels following confirmation at the parish church. He spent two hours in conversation with the Sisters--his first visit in eight years. We didn't know it then, but hope was on the horizon.

25.
The Finger of God

In 1889, with Father Daly gone for good, we welcomed the new pastor of Shelbyville, Father Crane. He, seeing the spiritual need of us all, invited two Jesuits from Saint Louis University for a week's mission to his congregation. Father Ward and Father J. I. Coghland, S. J., soon became acquainted with us and our history. They were intrigued, they said. Never having heard of our Order before, they made inquiries from friends and enemies, from the monks at Gethsemane and from Father Crane who had known us for years, and from Father Drury and other clergymen.

No sentimentalists, these practical and experienced missioners were nevertheless won over enthusiastically to our cause.

"What an astounding story!" Father Ward said. "Why it's almost unbelievable. From its simple, yet almost fantastic origin right down to today, it fascinates me."

Father Coghland said, "Except for the powerful grace of God, you couldn't have survived such trials. Dear Sisters, we assure you we are going to do everything we can to save this Order because we believe the finger of God has designed a great and beautiful future pattern for you."

When he spoke of the finger of God, I remembered how the enthusiastic Irish abbot, Dom Bruno Fitzpatrick, had used the same expression about us so many years before.

Father Coghland chuckled when he told of one parishioner saying, "Father Daly told us the Sisters were trying to poison him, putting broken glass into the Mass wine. Why," he broke out laughing, "Father Daly said he found it exuding through his forehead."

The two priests said, "Make no further appeals to Archbishop Elder. You need another field for your zealous activities. Work in another diocese."

These good fathers had contacts in the Middle West where they had been giving missions. They assured us that in the western dioceses there were demands for teaching orders.

Father Coghland especially worked on our behalf, writing letters of new opportunities. Once he wrote of an opportunity in Lincoln, Nebraska, under Bishop Bonacum. Later he wrote that our future lay in the diocese of Dubuque in Iowa where Bishop Hennessy was urging a broad program of education in his diocese. He influenced his friend, Father Roger Ryan, the vicar-general of Dubuque.

Bishop Hennessy suspected an Order that wished suddenly to abandon its home and transplant itself to a strange diocese. His replies to Mother Agnes were slow and evasive. He also feared antagonizing Bishop McCloskey, it turned out.

At last he invited Mother Agnes and a companion to come to Dubuque for interviews, providing we had permission from Bishop McCloskey. Bishop McCloskey hesitated on account of our debts. Nobody wanted to buy our heavily mortgaged property in the dying town of Shelbyville.

Bishop Hennessy cordially received Mother Agnes and Sister Assissium in April, 1890. For two hours they talked. The bishop was vague as to which schools he would assign us, but he promised he would accommodate us.

Still Bishop McCloskey refused. We agonized and waited. Then his letter of "exeant," or permission to leave, came. Rather ingraciously couched and his reluctance showing, he still did it. Then, in a few days, this surprising man of God, reverting to his former spirit of generosity, insisted on helping us unravel our snarled financial affairs in Shelbyville. He even took over mortgaged property so his business agent could dispose of it, he remitted some of our debts to the diocese, and he advanced money from his slender purse so we could meet our pressing needs. May God remember his benevolence in eternity. But, our other debts, would not be paid until after years of earning in Iowa.

Mother Agnes called in her councillors, as we prepared to leave for Iowa in the autumn of 1890.[28] She said to me, "You are the pioneer member of our Order, dear Sister Frances. You are one of our founders. You had perilous adventures and suffering before I entered. Are we doing the right thing? There is danger and uncertainty ahead."

But I and every member of the community fervently pledged our loyalty to her and to our Order in this "Iowa adventure." And, we all renewed our vows to our holy father, Saint Francis.

Back in the fall of 1889, we had suffered a severe epidemic of typhoid fever in Shelbyville. Death visited many a home and the convent of Our Lady. Since there were few nurses in the city, when our Sisters volunteered to care for the sick we were gladly accepted, by both Protestants and Catholics. For the first time in our history, the Shelbyville newspapers carried laudatory articles on the work of our nuns. Now, during our preparations for leaving, the fever raged again-- July to October, 1890. Nearly half our community came down with it, but none died. However, our departure for Dubuque was delayed until December 2nd for all but the twelve Sisters who had escaped the fever. They went on in late September because Bishop Hennessy's priests needed teachers for their schools.

26.
Owls at Olivet

We could bear to give up our other schools when we left for Iowa, but we wanted to keep Mount Olivet. That grand old monk and saint, Abbot Benedict, our friend and patron, died in August of 1890. His successor, Abbot Edward Chaix-Bourbon, was a man of a different stripe. During his short regime, Gethsemane did not prosper. He was amiable, but wanted us to leave.

We couldn't be forced to go, as we now had a vested right in the property. But we five nuns remaining at Olivet knew our doom was sealed when Bishop McCloskey wrote Mother Agnes saying, "The present abbot will have nothing to do with the school on the hill. I think you would do well to bring the Sisters of Mount Olivet with you . . ."

Abbot Edward offered us five hundred dollars for the property. We accepted, giving up our claim to it. We sold our furniture and live stock and closed the school the last of November.

We stood on the veranda of the great hall that last afternoon. The fields were quiet. The hills lay dark green with winter. The laughter of children still echoed in these halls for me. My throat was tight and my eyes were full.

"Cheer up, Sisters," said Sister Michael. "Our consolation is that we had our greatest enrollment in these last years. During these four years many a poor girl has received technical training and religious instruction she never would have enjoyed."

"My consolation," I said, "is that dear old Abbot Benedict, my friend of thirty years and my father's friend, died before these doors closed. We were his god-children in religion. This was the work so dear to his heart."

After we left, Gethsemane Abbey itself went through its worst crisis. The new abbot installed a friend of his from Chicago, Illinois, in our farmhouse--a visionary lady who was nursing what appeared to be stigmata. Later he tried to use Mount Olivet as a school for boys who couldn't afford

Gethsemane College. He appointed a principal who posed as an English nobleman and whose shady affairs almost ruined Mount Olivet School and Gethsemane College.

By 1903 the roofs and walls leaked and cattle wandered into the ground-floor rooms. But the next superior, the renowned abbot, Dom Edmond Albrecht, brought to Mount Olivet a brief glory. The buildings were cleaned up to house an order of Cistercian monks. The brothers, welcomed from France, had been expelled from their country during the hectic war waged against the Church by George Clemanceau and his anticlerical friends. For two years these exiled French Trappists settled there and chanted the office in the chapel where we had sung our hymns. They worked in the charming gardens where we and the children had walked and laughed and prayed.

But that last moment of glory of our once lovely home has vanished long ago. The last I heard of it, it was a pile of ruins on a lonely, wind-swept hill. I was told that at night this place resounded with the hoot of owls who flew in and out among the shadows. The souls of Sister Jane de Chantal and Abbot Benedict are among the blessed, I know, but I wonder if, while they tarried in purgatory, they mourned over the destruction and the desolation of the once beautiful Mount Olivet.

PART TWO
Iowa

27.
A Welcome and a Challenge

I still have a rather bewildered picture in my mind of the scenes of our departure from Kentucky. It was a time of mixed emotions--of confusion, of apprehension about an insecure future, of sadness and also of gaiety. Most of our Sisters were still young enough to see humorous twists in the quirks that Fortune was playing with us. I thanked God for that, for it was a sad enough affair.

We arranged with Mother Agnes to have the bodies of our deceased Sisters brought from Mount Olivet, from Chicago Hill and from Shelbyville to be buried in the Sisters' lot in Saint Louis Cemetery in Louisville before we left. Although the Shelbyville convent had been the home of suffering for many years, sadness tugged at our hearts as we saw the place stripped and bare, all its furniture gone. Even the altar was removed from our beloved old chapel.

In September we heard that our first twelve Sisters--the ones who had escaped the fever--had arrived in Dubuque. "Twelve apostles," they called themselves. Bishop Hennessy had written that his priests were impatient to have them for the September term.

Our Sisters wrote of their kind reception by the Franciscan nuns of Saint Francis Industrial School near Dubuque. Some of those warm-hearted welcomers were Iowans, but half of them were brown-habited Franciscans-- immigrants fifteen years earlier from Germany.

Four of our Sisters were almost immediately sent to tiny Vail in Western Iowa, three hundred miles from Dubuque. The other eight, under Sister Dolorosa, had to wait until mid October when their house would be completed in Mason City, in Northern Iowa.

During these weeks of waiting in Dubuque, Bishop Hennessy showed himself extremely cordial, but never again after that!

Meanwhile our Sisters from Shelbyville slowly recovered from typhoid fever. We gathered in Louisville December first. That night some of us stayed with the Sisters of Mercy and others with the Ursulines. The next morning we left Kentucky forever.

Two days and one night we were on the railroad journey. We were too poor for a Pullman, so what sleeping we did was on the benches. Most of us had never been out of Kentucky. We talked of our unknown future on that long train ride and made a pet of Carlos, the huge Saint Bernard Mother Agnes had brought from Fancy Farm.

We thought we were going to have a battle to keep Carlos with us on the train. A fatherly-looking old conductor and a grinning gold-toothed black porter attempted politely-worded objections to having a dog in a passenger section. But they were smothered by arguments from the younger Sisters.

The problem was settled by our promise that Florence Gillim was to be the constant, careful custodian of Carlos during the journey. Florence was the sixteen-year-old postulant who had won her parent's consent to go with us. She still carried her long curls and wore civilian dress.

We were absolutely ignorant of our Iowa destination except that its name was Anamosa and it was the site of a state reformatory!

A crowd had gathered at the Illinois Central Station when we pulled into Dubuque. Many had gathered to take our train west to Sioux City and Omaha. Gusts of snow blew about, but the setting sun sent an occasional golden streak through the thin snow clouds.

Father Roger Ryan, the vicar-general, and his driver, Con Shea the cathedral sexton, awaited us with a huge sleigh--a sort of bob sled--drawn by four draft horses. We climbed in with our baggage and for the first time became acquainted with buffalo robes which we spread over our knees.

On our way to the mother house of the Dubuque Franciscan Sisters, Father Ryan announced we would first drive past the cathedral rectory. Bishop Hennessy came out hatless.

"And what have you there, Father Ryan?" he called out.

Father Ryan, sitting on the driver's seat with the sexton, laughed and called back: "Some nuns, a girl and a dog!"

Twenty nuns, Florence, and Carlos. Florence wore a gray traveling suit and a sailor hat which the snowy gusts tried to blow off! Carlos, the only sure 'nuff saint in the bunch, stood up, waving his long frond-like tail, extending his nose toward the bishop.

A Welcome and a Challenge 127

"How many nuns?" asked the bishop.

"Twenty, your lordship," called Father Ryan.

The bishop bowed and turned back to his residence. We drove on to the convent at the north end of the city.

We couldn't have received a kinder, warmer welcome than we received from Dubuque Franciscan superior, Mother Xavier, and her nuns. But, it turned out Anamosa was not ready for us, so we stayed on as guests of our Dubuque friends until January. Our Sister Roberta sprained her ankle and stayed until February.

On the day after our arrival, Mother Agnes and Sister Magdalen called on Bishop Hennessy. They came back down-cast. Sister Magdalen told me later, "Bishop Hennessy has lost his cordiality. He acted like an icicle." He spoke of having directed Father Robert Powers, the pastor at Anamosa, to make some sort of provision for a mother house for us at Anamosa, and showed little interest in our affairs. In our short interview, he acted as if he wanted to wash his hands of our community. His coldness mystified us."

Later we learned that Bishop Hennessy and Mother Agnes had taken an instant dislike of each other. Even more alarming, the bishop spoke of having our order joined with the Dubuque community. "After all," he said to Father Johannes, spiritual director of the Dubuque Franciscans, "both orders are Franciscans of the Third Order and both follow the same Rule."

Both Mother Agnes and Mother Xavier refused the plan.

I listened with intense interest one evening at the table as Mother Xavier of the Dubuque Franciscans narrated the story of her Order. We loved the delay over our coffee, for our "pauper's diet" in Kentucky had eliminated the luxury of coffee!

Mother Xavier's community had started partly in Alsace-Lorraine but actually in Hereford, Germany, about the time Aunt Caroline Warren commenced our order at Gethsemane. These German Franciscans nursed in army hospitals and also cared for orphans. In the Austro-Prussian War they nursed in army hospitals. In 1870 in the Franco-German War, they accompanied field hospitals to the front. Two nuns died in lazarettes (field medical stations).[29] After the war the Empress Augusta had bestowed the Iron Cross, a war decoration of great distinction, upon the order.

"But this honor," laughed Mother Xavier, "didn't prevent them from expelling us a few years later when we resisted

Chancellor Bismarck during his war against the Church. Such is the gratitude of princes!"

The Franciscan exiles arrived in Iowa City in 1875. Surviving struggles as fierce as our own, they were now securely and prosperously settled and enjoying a new commodious mother house in Dubuque.

It being definitely determined now that our Kentucky order would retain its identity, Father Robert Powers came up from Anamosa to inspect us. Tousle-haired, broad-chested and stentorian-voiced, Father Powers was a joy to see and hear. He loved dogs. He often had a half-dozen homeless hounds following at his heels in Anamosa. He made up with Carlos right away, but he didn't take to Mother Agnes.

Sparks flew between Father Powers and Mother Agnes from their very first meeting. He roared Shakespearean English and wrote barbed letters to most of us, but not to Mother Agnes.

"You led me to understand, Reverend Mother," he rumbled, "that you made definite, clear arrangements with the bishop. But when I asked your first group of Sisters, they couldn't tell me anything. It seemed amazing to me that a dozen Sisters should migrate to Iowa with so little information. It looked like walking out into darkness. What good can be gained by keeping everybody blindly ignorant?"

"You could have learned by consulting Bishop Hennessy," Mother Agnes snapped.

"I didn't," said Father Powers, "because I had neither time nor means to travel fifty miles to pry into whatever transpired between his lordship and you."

"But you surely knew twenty more of us Sisters were coming to Iowa," insisted Mother Agnes.

"I had so many conflicting directions," said Father Powers, "that I was confounded. Now, permit me to do what you would not do--to tell the whole truth. Our school attendance isn't large at Anamosa. One competent teacher could take charge of it. Twenty incompetents may make it a failure. Comparison and competition will come from the public school, the pride of Protestant Anamosa. There every teacher holds a first class certificate. We must win certificates, then challenge and surpass them. Religion must not be an excuse for mediocrity--a poor substitute for secular education--especially within sight of a state agency, the Iowa State Reformatory!"

A Welcome and a Challenge

Father Powers was a task master, but we liked his challenge. Not so Mother Agnes. Her dislike grew during the following years to hatred, almost.

28.
Anamosa

A ray of sunshine during our first month in Iowa was the reception of five of our sisters to teach at Petersville under Sister Magdalen. Father Peter O'Dowd escorted them from Dubuque by train and sleigh. Through the ten-below-zero cold they went--a shocking change from Kentucky. But the last four miles they heard the church bells pealing out a welcome. They found the convent, elegantly furnished and comfortably heated by a steam furnace. The women of the parish prepared a warm and bountiful feast.

The rest of us left the warm charity of the Dubuque Franciscans to enter the cold, partially-prepared buildings at Anamosa which served as our mother house. Father Powers reminded us in many ways that he had never wanted us. He had originally hoped to install another community of nuns. He constantly declaimed the necessity of "challenging and surpassing" the public school teachers. We were able to satisfy him on this score, but the climate was tense.

Our school was an old brick church originally, with a special part fitted for music and art rooms. We lived in a one story cottage for three years. In these cramped and unsanitary quarters, we put up beds every night in odd corners.

An old stable on the grounds became our dormitory in summer. We rented sleeping rooms from neighbors. And, across the street, we could see the inmates parading the grounds of the state reformatory.

One sunny but cool day in late October of 1891, I came from the stable to enter the cottage. Here rose two smiling but travel-worn ladies.

"Aren't you Sister Frances?" they asked.

"Yes," I said, "and I think I know you! Dyer! Misses Dyer!"

"We are, and wasn't your mother Isabelle Cambron? We bring greetings from the Baltimore Cambrons."

"Oh, wonderful!" I said. "I haven't heard from them or about them in ages. Please sit down and tell me who is which and what you are going to teach here."

"I am Cecelia Anne," said the older one. "I majored in music at college and I was teaching music and literature in the Baltimore schools. I understand I am to continue with those courses here. I resigned my position back there only two weeks ago."

"I'm Agnes," said the younger. "Agnes Mudd Dyer. I graduated from the Normal a year ago and am to teach elementary classes."

"Agnes Mudd?" I asked, surprised. "Then you are..."

"Yes, you've guessed it," they laughed in answer. "We are nieces of that notorious character, Dr. Samuel A. Mudd."

"Notorious, indeed!" I said indignantly, and then I saw their eyes twinkling.

"Well, Sister," they explained, "you know he was arrested and imprisoned for a time. But his case was dismissed. We think he's a charming and lovable uncle."

How often we Sisters had discussed the case of Dr. Samuel Mudd and John Wilkes Booth. Booth, the actor, broke his leg leaping to the stage after he shot Lincoln. Dr. Mudd attended him and set the leg. In the hysteria following Lincoln's death, Dr. Mudd was accused of conspiring in the assassination plot, but he was declared innocent. Now, here were the daughters of Mary Clare Mudd, Dr. Samuel's sister, as teachers in our Anamosa academy.

Mother Agnes selected Sister Carmel and several other "geniuses" of our community to make up the school's faculty. In addition she had the two imported Misses Dyers. Thus Father Powers' ultimatum was answered with a vengeance. Our academy "challenged and surpassed" every school in the Anamosa area.

The Dyer sisters shared our poverty and misery with us. They slept in crowded corners. They were as brave and cheerful as the rest, and on a salary of thirty dollars a month. When we later moved to Clinton, they continued for a time to teach in our academy. They would later be prominent matrons in the religious and social life of Baltimore.

Father Powers frowned at the surprising number of postulants. Young ladies came from various parts of Iowa. Our cottage, coach house and other outhouses could no longer shelter our members. Health was at risk.

John Green of nearby Stone City offered to donate stone to build a convent near the church on a lot belonging to

Father Powers. Mother Agnes seized on the proposal for the erection of a new mother house. The building was started and pushed, despite clashes between Mother and the pastor.

Halfway through construction, Father Powers decided to use part of it for a hospital. Dr. Gawley, a prominent local physician, argued that proceeds from the hospital could help pay for the building.

Mother Agnes objected. She didn't want novices mixed up with patients, doctors and nurses in such a public place as a hospital. Discussions, misunderstandings and ill feelings followed, as well as a widening breach between superior and pastor. These embroilments were laid before Bishop Hennessy. An unapproachably stern man, he also partook of Father Power's dislike for Mother Agnes.

In the spring of 1893, our Sisters allowed the entire building to be used as a sanatorium. They would continue living in our old crowded quarters. Four Sisters under Sister Dolorosa were placed in charge of the hospital.

Looking back, I thank God we didn't acquire the stone building for our mother house. We might have remained in Anamosa--a consummation that probably would have proved disastrous to our Sisterhood.

To please Bishop Hennessy when he started his ill-fated order of the Sisters of the Holy Ghost in Dubuque in 1891, we sent one of our highly trained nuns, Sister Xavier Ryan, to the new convent. Poor as we were, we gladly made the sacrifice. For several years of service by this Sister we received no compensation.

When Father Carolon from Mason City invited us to move our mother house there, we leaped to answer his invitation. We had little compensation from Anamosa. Our only income came from the music class and our few mission schools. But, Father Carolon capriciously withdrew his offer and left us disappointed.

Then, several of our best novices, advised by Father Powers, left our community and entered the convent of the Sisters of Mercy in nearby Cedar Rapids.

Then a number of our best postulants left. They saw no future in our "Bee Hive" cottage. The State Reformatory below us loomed up as a daily spectre of gloom. Our Sisters had recurring illnesses. Our community again plunged into debt. One day one of the suffering Sisters said, "We were better off in the poverty of Shelbyville than we've been here."

No generous Bishop McCloskey or benevolent Abbot Benedict came forward with aid. Bishop Hennessy kept aloof from our problems--and from Mother Agnes.

If Father Powers was officious, Mother Agnes was tyrannical. Indeed, from her arrival in Iowa she was a new Mother Agnes. Furtive and close-lipped in her dealings with us of the community, she developed friends among clergy in Indiana and Illinois. They became her counselors. She cultivated friendship with socially prominent families in Iowa. Other Sisters and I became uneasy. What was happening to our once peerless and fearless Kentucky leader?

29.
The Duel

I missed some of those hectic days at Anamosa for I had gone to open a small school in the hamlet of Keystone. This little Catholic school made a brave beginning, struggled for a while, then closed. This was the history of many of our pioneer schools in Iowa. Bishop Hennessy was a forcible advocate of parochial schools in the smallest outposts. But many in sparsely settled rural districts could not survive.

But when I returned from Keystone I felt quite happy because I had brought with me two pious and talented young ladies who would later become outstanding Sisters in our community. All was not lost with the closing of a school.

I learned of an experimental opening of Saint Patrick's School in Clinton, Iowa. Father J. A. Murray asked for five Sisters. Sister Rose and four others went to the little stone convent at Saint Patrick's in September of 1891.

When I returned to Anamosa at the end of August, 1893, Sister Carmel met me at the door of the cottage. "Dear Sister Frances," she said, "let me be the first to tell you the big news. Have you heard?"

"No, I've heard nothing," I answered.

"We're moving our Mother House to Clinton!"

"We are?" I asked. "When? How did that come about?"

"Principally through the influence of Father Murray," she said. "You see, he found a splendid piece of property in the western part of Clinton, not far from his church. I'm told we paid only six thousand dollars--a splendid bargain."

She saw my face. "Oh, there'll be a mortgage on it," she said, "but don't worry about that. The big problem was to gain Bishop Hennessy's consent. That was gained only through the enthusiastic efforts of Father Murray!"

"But," I persisted, "how will we pay the mortgage?"

"Don't worry," she said, "about the money. We're going to have an academy for both day pupils and boarders in connection with the mother house. We're going to start right in. We're moving to Clinton in two weeks--all but a few of us Sisters."

"Heavens," I exclaimed, "it must be quite a place."

"It's a three story brick building on five acres. Everybody knows the place--it's called the Judge Chase property. I saw it in Clinton last week. It'll seem like a mansion after this cottage."

"A comfortable home," I thought, "after three years crammed into the Anamosa cottage and outbuildings."

"Father Powers stormed over here this morning," Sister Carmel said with a giggle. "He was furious over our leaving. You could hear him all over the house--his booming voice, his musical roar. Oh, he complained! Said, we hadn't treated him right!"

I looked around at the cottage and out the window at the coach house. These buildings had been a convent, a novitiate, and a music conservatory. He hadn't considered provisions for the new postulants. Yet, we hadn't treated him right. "How did he dare?" I asked.

"Too true," said Sister Carmel, "but we mollified him somewhat before he left. We're leaving four Sisters here at the cottage to conduct the school, and four others to conduct Father's hospital."

Since the Clinton property was purchased on August 12th, the Feast of Saint Clare, and it stood high on a graceful elevation, we named it Mount Saint Clare.[30] We erected a large cross on the convent.

I was happily present when the formal opening and blessing of the institution took place, October 4th, 1893, the feast of our Father, Francis of Assisi. Clinton's Dean E. J. McLaughlin performed the ceremony, assisted by Father Murray and other clergymen. Dean McLaughlin blessed a bell which we hung in the tower.

Thus began a new era of prosperity for our community. We now felt we had a home and, with God's blessings and hard work, we would pay for it.

Meanwhile at Anamosa Father Powers made demands on our nuns which they couldn't meet. He still raged over the removal of our mother house. Father Powers, the Sisters and Dr. Gawley wrangled over hospital affairs. As a result we withdrew all our Sisters in the summer of 1894. The school closed and the hospital administration went to the Sisters of Mercy of Cedar Rapids. Sister Michael had died while we were at Anamosa, so we brought her body from Anamosa to Clinton for reburial in the Catholic cemetery.

The Duel

The duel between Mother Agnes and Father Powers dragged on, irritatingly and amusingly. The priest's letters, still preserved in my portfolio are literary masterpieces. Some bristle with acrimony and others are full of profound Christian charity.

In the fall of 1894 Father Powers wrote:

"Dear Mother,

"Replying to your last letter permit me to say that I wish I could believe you that all our school ledgers were 'destroyed' (whatever this means) in the unpacking of the good Sisters at Clinton.

"However, we must have them: that's all. Without more than your word I can't see the remotest possibility of our coming to anything like a just settlement of accounts. At first you claimed and distinctly said there was an indebtedness of yours here of $900.00. Next it was revised and footed up (as) $533.00. The third attempted revision brought it down to $329.00. I make no doubt a half-dozen more accurate divisions and subtractions will continue to reduce the sum due in the same ratio of progression. It may not appear brilliant, much less honest, to be advertised abroad of 'holy religious' that 900=533=329 . . zero; but I can see no help for it.

"What in this world, or in the next did you hope to gain by taking away these ledgers and Sunday School books--things which are not yours? Little things that would never make anyone the richer, and are worthy of notice only to show the mind that snatches them. You may challenge this statement, if you will: I am ready.

"It will be a great consolation to you to know that other Sisters are in charge of the hospital. You remember how fervently you 'wished to God I would send the Franciscans home as you could use them to much greater advantage elsewhere.' Now you will have the consummation so devoutly wished. No doubt you will be very glad of it, and thank and bless and pray for me. Although I have lost more in many ways by your coming to Anamosa than I may expect to regain in a lifetime, yet I shall always have nothing but good will for you, and yours. I shall leave the past altogether in the hands of Him Who doth all things well. Our parting may be lasting and long until we meet at the tribunal where each shall receive due need for the deed done in the flesh.

"Mindful of that awful future let us straighten up our little material differences here. Let me have those books that should never have been removed from here. What good in delaying? Do you think that I have time to waste in foolish correspondence like this? Isn't one document of this kind as good as a thousand? Why not give the miserable matter immediate attention? I have made this same request, in word or writing, at least a score of times before; how often again must I make it? It is for you to say."

"Faithfully yours,

"Rob't Powers."

30.
Archbishop Forces Election

Divine Providence continued to bless us with good vocations--devout young women coming into our community. During our first ten years after Kentucky, most of our new Sisters came from Iowa, as was natural. Our first novice at Anamosa, Cynthia Murcher from Saint Mary's parish of Dubuque, was admitted in June of 1891. She took the name of Sister Angelico and worked enthusiastically, faithful to God, until her death twenty-three years later.

The Kentuckians continued to come, some from my old home area of Marion County and others from Whitesville and Fancy Farm.

We succeeded in our very first year at Mount Saint Clare. The original brick building, spacious as it was, soon became too small to accommodate the growing number of Sisters and boarders.

Mother Agnes persuaded the newly elevated Archbishop Hennessy to permit the erection of a large addition to Mount Saint Clare. We moved into the new wing in September, 1895.

But now we lived under the shadow of mortgaged property again. She'd borrowed twelve thousand dollars at six percent interest, which we paid on for thirteen years!

Now came times that approached the harsh poverty of Shelbyville. Boarding students didn't increase as expected for our enlarged academy. Debts increased alarmingly. Some mission schools prospered, but others faltered. We even opened a school across the river at Kickapoo, Illinois, which flourished for a time.

However, it took all the income from our missions to pay the interest on our debts. We were still trying to pay back something on debts in Kentucky. Again, we Sisters lived on credit. Bills multiplied all over Clinton until that embarrassing time came when merchants refused to grant us credit.

We older Sisters suspected that the problem was management. The archbishop and the priests learned how things were mismanaged, so they had little sympathy for us. But, we were governed by an autocrat. We, the Sisters, were not consulted and could not be responsible for the decisions and mistakes of Mother Agnes.

Mother Agnes raised money, nevertheless. She raffled off an organ and watch and raised two thousand dollars. A bazaar, or "Kermess" brought another five thousand. But this money couldn't reduce our mortgages. We had to have it to meet current expenses.

Mother Agnes' methods drew fire from other priests besides Father Powers. By 1897 so many complaints had reached Archbishop Hennessy that he called for a copy of our Rule. He was curious about Mother Agnes' re-election every three years since 1878. There must be regulations for the election of the mother general and other officers of our Order.

The archbishop's investigation clued us in to his suspicions. After examining our Rule and statutes, he authorized the Very Reverend Dean McLaughlin to inform Mother Agnes she could not be a candidate. The law of the Church required that all superiors of religious houses must go out of office every six years.

However, instead of carrying out the archbishop's orders and informing the Sisters, Mother Agnes remained silent. She allowed herself to be re-elected at the close of our retreat. Into our protocol she wrote, simply:

"The Franciscan, Father Clement, O.F.M., conducted the retreat this month, August, 1897. At its close, the election of Mother Superior took place at which Reverend Mother Agnes was re-elected. The votes were sent in to the Archbishop but he returned them without his approval."

Archbishop Hennessy sternly refused to recognize the validity of the election, yet Mother Agnes held office in spite of this. Long after this, when we had a number of postulants to be invested, Archbishop Hennessy refused to grant Mother Agnes permission to have the reception. From this time on, he ignored the community. He didn't allow novices to make their vows until long after their term of probation had expired. Still, Mother Agnes held on to the office.

Now Mother Agnes had religious dress put on postulants and they were sent out to missions to teach. Some became discouraged and left without understanding why they couldn't receive their habits. Novices rebelled. No one explained why they were kept three or four years in the novitiate. Some of these gave up and left the community.

"Why, oh why, Sister Frances, do these things have to happen to us?" cried Sister Magdalen to me.

It seems strange to me today that I could not answer. But it was not strange then. Mother Agnes was a saintly, powerful woman. It seemed as if she were the savior of our Order. Under her leadership we had emerged from the valley of suffering. She had led us from Egypt and brought us through the Red Sea of misfortune into the promised land of Iowa. We didn't know about the way she managed because she didn't tell us.

The few of us older Sisters who knew something of what was going on dared not discuss what we did know. When she refused our pleas about the election, we feared challenging her publicly. There would be a scandal and life for us in the community would be intolerable.

I knew too well the sorrowful Way of the Cross of our Order. With the exception of the gentle Mother Jane de Chantal, every superior had, when voted out, publicly abandoned us or resigned. Was history to repeat itself?

Sister Magdalen was begging for an answer. "Why, why?"

Suddenly the spectre of my fears resolved itself into a kindly light.

"Come into the chapel with me, Sister Magdalen," I said, taking her arm. "Let us pray and have good cheer. I know, I tell you, that the end is in sight."

I am no believer in the preternatural, but I seemed to have a sudden feeling of confidence in God's mercy and power.

"He whom the Lord loveth, He chastiseth," I quoted. "He has chastised us a long time, but now He's going to show His love for us in a different way."

The answer soon came.

A large and valuable property, the Corbin estate, convenient to Mount Saint Clare, came up for sale in April of 1899. Mother Agnes quickly secured it for six thousand dollars. A large, handsome brick house, brick barn and other buildings stood on the land. We immediately used it for our novices' residence and named it Mount Alverno after Saint Francis' mountain retreat of La Verna near Assisi.

Our community now owed eighteen thousand on real estate at six percent. Besides that we had floating debts of perhaps more than ten thousand--big money for those years.

We held another "Kermess" or bazaar in the new land and took in sixteen hundred dollars. This pacified only our most insistent creditors.

Yet the throbs of these financial headaches were gentle pulsations compared to the spasms created by the archbishop's interdict. He returned our letters unopened. No longer, he said, could we receive "subjects," as he put it. A pall hung over our community.

One morning shortly after New Year's of 1900, the best of our class of postulants marched to Mother Agnes' office. Full of devout courage, they laid out their case. "Investiture this very month, dear Mother, or we leave the Mount on our confessor's strict advice!"

Mother Agnes, apprehensive of her position, sent Sister Dolorosa and Sister Xavier to Dubuque to wait on his grace. Archbishop Hennessy opened by expressing his indignation at Mother Agnes' defiance. He said, "What I further cannot understand is the outrageous disobedience of you Sisters by keeping Mother Agnes in office, not merely contrary to my wishes, but in utter defiance of the expressed law of the Church." He paused for breath. "I will have nothing to do with you while you keep that woman in office."

"We wish to assure your grace," said Sister Dolorosa, "that we Sisters never, never wished to defy your authority. We are ready and willing to carry out your orders."

"Well, madam," he answered, "all I ask you to do is simply this: elect a superior legally! I would like you to understand that your present superior is holding office under false pretenses, that she is not recognized by me and that for several years she has been in office by insolently setting at naught the laws of the Church."

"We understand your wishes, your grace," said Sister Dolorosa, "and we are sure that Mother Agnes does also by this time."

"Let me assure you, madam," he said as he accompanied the Sisters to the door, "until you elect a superior according to law, I will not recognize your Order as belonging to my archdiocese nor will I have any dealings whatsoever with you."

In the meantime Mother Agnes, thinking she had found a loophole to gain delay, hastily sent Sister Magdalen and another Sister to the vicar general, Father Ryan in Dubuque. Her petition was for Father Ryan to use his influence on the archbishop to postpone the election until the following summer when all the Sisters would return to the mother house.

Father Ryan was as adamant as the archbishop. He knew he was dealing with a determined woman and advised, "Go home, dear Sisters, and hold your election immediately. Otherwise you'll be neither blessed nor recognized."

Years have passed. I am a very old lady now who will soon appear before her God. I want to be gentle, but I must tell the truth. Mother Agnes heard the messages from the archbishop and the vicar general, but she held on to office.

I pitied her then. She imperiled the existence of our Order. She proposed to us older Sisters that we send Sisters to Washington to interview the Apostolic Delegate and enlist his sympathies. We resisted this proposition, knowing it would mean more trouble.

"Appeal to the Delegate," I asked, "and have him send this case to Rome? Think of our past history at Mount Olivet and Shelbyville. Our troubles have reached Rome before. If this matter goes to Rome our community will be suppressed!"

Mother Agnes announced the next day that the election would take place January 27, 1900, and that she was not a candidate.

That we were happy and relieved did not mean that we were ungrateful for what Mother Agnes had done. We had been loyal to her and had prayed for her because we had honored her. Now we knew we must move to new leadership. In fact, several Sisters dubbed the election announcement as the "Emancipation Proclamation."

31.
Interrupted Election

On the 27th of January, 1900, we elected Sister Mary Magdalen Mattingly as Mother Superior. Twenty Sisters cast their ballots while Father Murray presided.[31]

We elected Mother Agnes as the first of four consultors and Mother Magdalen graciously appointed her assistant mother and, later, mistress of novices. But, this well-intended gesture would prove to be a mistake.

Immediately after Mother Magdalen was installed, all of the postulants were, at last, invested and a number of novices made their first vows. In less than two months, Archbishop John Hennessy died.

Sister Angelico, after hearing of his death, remarked, "Wasn't it providential that this iron-willed churchman lived long enough?"

What a shift of our mood from 1900 on! One day, coming out of the community room, little Sister Paschal eagerly took my hand. "There seems," she said, "to be such a profound change in our convent now. Don't you truthfully think, Sister Frances, that the grace of God is working wonders amongst us now?"

"Yes," I agreed. "I don't believe, in all my years, I've seen such peace, such kindliness in the entire Order. Now that we have the Church's blessing again, we realize how much we've missed."

"Now," said Sister Paschal, "I feel I could face any kind of storm without fear."

During the next six years, we paid our floating debts, we restored our Clinton credit, and our Sisters walked in public unashamed. We acquired twenty-five acres adjoining Mount Alverno and promptly paid for it.

Our mission schools at Hawarden, Iowa, and Toluca, Illinois, prospered. The income enabled Mother Magdalen to reduce the mortgages on Mount Saint Clare.

We acquired a new hospital in Macomb, Illinois. We did it with the encouragement of Macomb's Father F. J. Lantz, and the assistance of Dr. Joseph Bacon, Macomb's leading surgeon. But we borrowed the money at heavy interest. Hospital equipment and furniture cost a fortune, secular nurses at first failed us, and the city was, at first strongly non-Catholic.

We spared as many Sisters as we could, but few had the inclination or talent for a hospital. But the faith of those who served was a joy and eventually brought success.

In 1903 Mother Agnes ran for re-election but failed. We again elected Mother Magdalen superior. She in turn appointed Mother Agnes as assistant and as mistress of novices.

Next year we added another wing to Mount Saint Clare and paid cash. All seemed serene at the end of six years with Mother Magdalen.

Father Murray had received written appointment to preside at the election on January 27, 1906, the election when Mother Magdalen's second term would expire. Then he received a long distance telephone call from Archbishop Keane, Archbishop Hennessy's successor, directing him to cancel the election. It seemed that Archbishop Keane had received word that a letter of complaints against the Sisters of Mount Saint Clare had been delivered to the Papal Delegate in Washington, D.C.

Father Murray quickly canceled the election and prepared for a hurried episcopal visit. [32]

Archbishop Keane, one of the founders and the first rector of the Catholic University of America, wrote Mother Magdalen on January 30th:

"I shall go down to Clinton next Friday, spend the night at Dean McLaughlin's and be at your convent Saturday morning, please God, about nine o'clock. You will assemble the community. After addressing them in a body, I will receive each Sister singly and hear what she has to say concerning her own spiritual welfare or the welfare of the community. Each one must not only feel perfectly free to speak to me plainly, but must feel bound in conscience to do so."

When Archbishop Keane arrived, he talked a long time that Friday evening with Dean McLaughlin and Father Murray. Both of these pastors were well acquainted with Mother Agnes. They gleaned enough from the archbishop's innocent questions to realize Mother Agnes had been seeking the Sisters' support to elect her again.

The priests assured the archbishop they knew of no trouble at the convent, that the Sisters were edifying, self-sacrificing and untiring in their labors in the churches and schools. All the pastors, they said would gladly testify to this.

The archbishop had feared the worst. As he rose from his chair for the night, he said in a ringing voice--he was a great pulpit orator--"Gentlemen, you have lifted a heavy burden from my mind!"

At Mount Saint Clare the next morning, we were all still ignorant of what the unusual proceedings might mean. We older Sisters had been called home for the investigation. The archbishop proved to be thorough but kind. Each Sister had a chance to open her heart to this saintly churchman and get his fatherly advice and blessing. After the long, strange day of interviews, we assembled in the chapel. It was a happy archbishop who addressed us.

"Seldom," he said, "have I ever found a spirit of charity and unity such as yours." He emphasized loyalty to the Mother Superior.

I could not help but feel sorry for my dear friend in religion of so many years, Sister Agnes. She looked as if she were cut to the heart by the Archbishop's appeal.

After celebrating the Blessed Sacrament and giving the benediction, Archbishop Keane commended our community. He would immediately and gladly send a favorable report to the Apostolic Delegate, he said.

His final act upon leaving was to announce the election for February 8th. He told us to send our votes in sealed envelopes to him personally at Dubuque.

32.
A Sad Lesson

We mailed our votes February 10th. Archbishop Keane promptly sent us the results. We had elected Sister Paul of the Cross as our new superior. Mother Paul had been Laura Carrico of Fancy Farm, Kentucky. She had studied in the school our Sisters conducted there in the 1880's.

Mother Paul appointed Sister Magdalen her assistant and Sister Teresa mistress of novices. Again we enjoyed six years of peace and prosperity.

After the election, Mother Agnes requested permission to go to a Chicago hospital for medical treatment. After treatment there, she took charge of a parochial school in Chicago Heights. Shortly after that we got word that she was starting a new foundation.

Mother Agnes returned briefly to Mount Saint Clare. After she left, four of our novices separated from our community. Puzzled at first, we became suspicious when one of the novices wrote Mother Paul, asking to be allowed to return. Then two more begged for re-admission.

Mother Paul of the Cross called the council to listen to the novices' story. Their tales were similar. They had been influenced to leave and join the new foundation started by Mother Agnes. They were kindly received and re-admitted, but we were made uneasy by the affair.

Soon after, Mother Agnes publicly asked pardon and promised to atone for damage.

"One blessed effect of this trouble," Sister Angelica once said, "is that all the members of our Order are praying more fervently than ever before."

It was true. We prayed daily for the healing of our community.

Then one day a layman and a priest wrote demanding the return of their donations made during Mother Agnes' leadership. They wanted to apply the money, they said, to support a certain new foundation.

Although we were under no obligation, legal or moral, to return these gifts, we raised the cash, partly by a loan, and refunded it to the donors.

Then, after we had slipped peacefully some distance into the New Year of 1907, Mother Agnes asked permission to write Archbishop Keane of Dubuque on an "important matter of conscience." Permission having been granted, it developed that she wished to have an interview. Archbishop Keane answered in letters to Mother Paul and Mother Agnes that he would be pleased to grant the interview in June.

Mother Paul accompanied Mother Agnes on this mysterious trip and Mother Agnes had a private discussion with the archbishop. His grace returned to the drawing room where Mother Paul was waiting. He sat down and said, "Dear Mother Paul, probably you know already that Mother Agnes has become very unhappy in your community. From what she related she assumes you are aware of this."

"Yes, your grace," said Mother Paul.

"She has an offer," he continued, "to open an independent religious house at Saint Agnes parish in Chicago at Chicago Heights. I understand it is a very good offer."

"May I inquire who made the offer?" asked Mother Paul.

"Yes, of course. The pastor of the parish. Mother Agnes showed me his letters and also, in fact, a note from Archbishop Quigley of Chicago. He would gladly receive the new community."

"The new community?" asked Mother Paul, surprised. "Who are comprising this new community?"

"Oh, Mother Agnes has assured me that she has already secured the consent of two of your Sisters to accompany her for this new foundation." (A minimum of three Sisters was necessary to make a foundation.)

While Mother Paul pondered this, Archbishop Keane said, "Don't you think this is a peaceable way of settling our troubles--to permit Mother Agnes for the good of her soul, for the good of the community, and for the good of Archbishop Quigley's diocese to accept this offer?"

"Whatever you advise, your grace," said Mother Paul. The departure of Mother Agnes would be significant. "Is my consent now sufficient?"

"No, Mother," said the archbishop. "You could call a meeting of your council and lay the matter before them. Whatever you and they agree upon, I will readily sanction."

Mother Paul did call the council and the Sisters agreed to permit Mother Agnes to depart. One of the Sisters Mother Agnes had counted on refused point blank to accompany

A Sad Lesson

her, but she then induced an older Sister, lately dissatisfied, to become the third member of the foundation.

Then Mother Paul of the Cross drew up a paper showing that all rights and claims to our community of Franciscan Sisters were renounced by the three departing nuns. She had them sign it in the presence of the council. Next she wrote a letter to Archbishop Quigley.

Before the three Sisters left, we heard rumors of how we had treated Mother Agnes unfairly. Even our own chaplain denounced us.

This was a sad lesson to me. I had known Sister Agnes longer than anyone else. She had been with me for two months in lovely Mount Olivet in 1873. She came to Shelbyville as a postulant in 1875. Thirty-two years she had spent in our community, and for twenty-two of those years she had been our superior. It was a warning to us to work out our salvation in fear and trembling, "lest after having preached to others, we ourselves may become a castaway."

33.
I Pray for Her Every Day

The bitter cross of our Mother Agnes struggle, scandalous as it was, proved a blessing in numerous ways. God had delivered us to a new freedom. Our untold numbers of prayers were answered. Never before had the members of our Order been so united in love and loyalty. And, in spite of losing a few friends, we had the strong hand of friendship offered right and left from lay people and priests.

One of our friends, old Father Robert Powers of Anamosa, wrote to us. I could almost hear his booming, musical voice as I read it.

"Anamosa, Iowa, July 16, 1907

"Mother Paul of the Cross
Clinton, Iowa

Dear Mother:
At one time when we all took a hand in digging a sod to plant the Franciscan tree in Iowa soil, I thought that perhaps Providence might have intended me to be a weak instrument in helping cultivate the growing tree, by the sweat of my face, by the sweat of my brain, and by the sweat of my soul. But it seems my pious thoughts turned out to be folly, if not <u>tom-foolery</u>. "Man proposes"--but God bursts his propositions higher than a kite. Was it Job, or some other old man, who squatted on a manure pile and sang through his nose, <u>Dominus dedit et Dominus abstulit. Sit nomen Domini benedictum.</u> (The Lord gives. The Lord takes away. Blessed be the name of the Lord.) I supposed I was the only one advancing in age and wisdom before God and men, but I noticed at your last visit that the whole gang of us are hoofing it along the path by which no woman hath returned, and it can't be long until our early plans and prospects of an inseparable friendliness will come to the husking time, and the well-built crib beyond the stars.

"Well, to come to more profane things: Sheriff Hogan (by no means regretfully) informed me last Sunday evening that my dear old Sister (in-law) had taken her flight across the Mississippi River and landed on the Chicago Heights to make herself a foundation stone of an institute whence angels will ascend and descend, like old man Jacob on the ladder, until her spiritual progeny become as numerous as the stars of Abraham. The news of my old friend's migration made me mingle my tears with the sheriff's; and the rain fell fast and heavy.

"The Omniscient God Who knoweth all, and doth all things for the best, will, I trust, at the Judgment Day, give me credit for having done the best I could to control Mother Agnes in the circumstances according to my lights. Looking back now I think matters might have been otherwise if I were not (like many of the humble Sisters) in the passive mood--our guilt was sins of omission. But then our foresight was not as good as our present hindsight. We are all fast advancing toward the tribunal where our little kinks will be thoroughly unravelled. We shall then know it all.

"One thing at least may be undoubtedly stated without fear of failure--as long as we are left in this vale of olives, the old recollections will serve to keep us more united in the ties of friendship, and may the same tie, eventually sanctified, bind us everlastingly in the land that is better than this. In the meantime, believe me, dear Mother Paul,
"Very faithfully yours,
"Rob't Powers."

I know I will be pardoned if I gently draw the curtain of charitable silence over most of the subsequent activities and wanderings of Mother Agnes. The foundation lasted three years. Financial difficulties and lack of harmony brought grave troubles to Chicago's Archbishop Quigley until he suppressed the foundation and ordered the community to disband.

Another letter from the apostolic delegate in Washington, D. C. questioned why we had allowed Mother Agnes to separate from our community. Here Mother Paul's careful documentation satisfied the cardinal. He saw Mother Agnes' signed statement witnessed by four members of our council. Mother Paul had the evidence that Mother Agnes had left of her own free will.

Poor Mother Agnes! I would hear echoes of her strange activities through the passing years. I'm sure she could write a more weirdly interesting story than the tale of the wandering Jew. She travelled from one diocese to another in the Midwest, then Colorado and New Mexico. The Franciscan Sisters of Graymoor, New York, rejected her application. Twice she was given charge of hospital foundations by unsuspecting bishops. Bankruptcy followed.

Her ability to gain the ears of churchmen in high places never failed her. Twice heads of religious orders and four times bishops or archbishops wrote us letters on her behalf, asking us to take her unto our bosoms. Twice these letters were accompanied by pleas of her own. The bishop's favorite argument was the parable of the return of the Prodigal Son. One churchman assured us that if we repaid her the several thousand dollars allegedly due her, she would no longer annoy our community.

Poor Mother Agnes! I so loved her as the heroine of our Kentucky days. Our arrival in Iowa witnessed the disintegration, year after year, of the moral idealism of her great soul. I know God will be merciful to her. I pray for her every day and I shall continue to do so as long as I live.

34.
I Want to Go to My Room

What a glorious march of triumph--triumph both of grace and of material achievement--from that historic 1906 'til now! The Iowa years from 1890 to 1906 had been pioneer years of struggle and hardship, but now in this post-World War year of 1920 our Sisters of the Third Order of Saint Francis have known peace and growth. As if we were conscious of a new era setting in, in that year of 1906 we had erected that new wing at Mount Saint Clare Academy. Seven thousand dollars and we paid for it immediately!
   Let me jot a few lines of how we were in 1906:
   Eighty-three members in our community.
   Three outstanding institutions:
      Mount Saint Clare Academy in Clinton
      Mount Alverno Home and property in Clinton
      Saint Francis Hospital in Macomb, Illinois
   Six missions with high school and grade school:
      Saint Ann's Academy, Vail, Iowa
      Saint Joseph's High School, Mason City, Iowa
      Saint Anthony's School, Hawarden, Iowa
      Saint Mary's School, Tama, Iowa
      Saint Joseph's School, Akron, Iowa
      Saint Joachim's Academy, Toluca, Illinois
   Then we also conducted six grade schools:
      Immaculate Conception School, Petersville, Iowa
      Saint Patrick's School and Sacred Heart School, in Clinton
      Saint John's School, Epworth, Iowa
      Saint Joseph's School, Cresco, Iowa
      Saint Paul's School, Macomb, Illinois

   Since then, what a growth! And, in 1907, our community became affiliated with the world body of Franciscans, securing the rights and benefits of all Franciscan orders. We took new schools and a few far-flung missions even in Missouri and Nebraska!

What pleased us senior Sisters the most, however, was having our home state of Kentucky beckon us back for a welcome to the six Sisters who opened Maysville school in 1910. We returned exactly a score of years since we had last looked at blue grass and tobacco fields of our old homes. We returned as members of a debt-free community--a good sensation. Despite improvements and purchases of new sites, we had paid our Iowa and Kentucky creditors. We breathed a fervent "*Deo Gratias!*" (Thank God!).

After Mother Paul's re-election in 1909, we launched our greatest expansion. We built a five-story Mount Saint Clare Academy, selling "bricks" for five hundred dollars apiece. The Carricos of Kentucky and others "bought" enough that when the cornerstone was laid, November 13, 1910, Bishop P. J. Muldoon could announce that the two hundred thousand dollar cost was paid. We placed in the cornerstone a photograph of the first band of our Order which came to Iowa in 1890.

I have from that time on been living in the new Mount Saint Clare. While this grand new building far eclipses the old one in style and furnishings, our old home at Mount Olivet is still in my memory. Happy and active days, now gone forever.

After Mother Paul's six years, Mother Magdalen Mattingly was again elected, in 1912. Bishop Davis visited us, escorted by Father Murray. When he stepped into his automobile to leave, Bishop Davis turned to a group of us and said, "Now that I know more of your story, dear Sisters, I can well understand why you regard good, old Father Murray here as your actual Clinton founder."

I spoke up and said, "He has been more than that, your Lordship. He has been our constant benefactor."

"Thanks for compliments, everybody," said Father Murray, his eyes sparkling as he stepped into his seat by the bishop. "But I do believe that I take more pride in this community of Sisters than they do themselves." We all laughed happily as they drove off.

Mother Paul was re-elected mother general in 1915 and 1918. Our numbers grew. The Carneys of Grinnell left a legacy, and, along with another including a gift of five acres, we bought the Grinnell Hospital. In September, 1918, we opened our tiny college department. Our Sisters earned degrees from Catholic University of America and we launched Mount Saint Clare Junior College. Our academy affiliated with Loyola University.

I Want to Go to My Room

I'll stop in my enumeration of blessings to admit these are minor triumphs by the world's standards. And we've had our share of tragedies. Our beloved chaplain suddenly plunged into mental illness. Twice we've had epidemics among the students. Sickness has closed the eyes of many of our Sisters.

But, as for me, I've never been so happy as now in my declining years. "God's in His Heaven and all's well with the world."

Now with two hundred Sisters, I'm confused trying to recognize the bright new faces. Once we were all daughters of Kentucky. Now our candidates come from Iowa and neighboring states. We still have a trickle flowing from Kentucky--I noticed we have another Carrico postulant. There was Mother Paul of the Cross Carrico, Nola, Minnie and Edna Carrico, all from Fancy Farm, Kentucky, Marie Carrico from Knottsville, Kentucky, and Rena Carrico from Doniphon, Missouri.

Then we received Miss Amalia Mader from Germany and Nora Ryan from Ireland on the same day. A group of seventeen came from Ireland in August of 1908, the next August another five and in May of 1910 came another three. From Newfoundland came five in 1914, eighteen in 1915, seventeen in 1916 and in this year of 1920 came nine more.

It was the 19th of June, 1868, that our first Sisters were professed. We could celebrate our fifty-fourth year of continuous life. November 23rd, 1864, my Aunt Caroline Warren, the original founder of our Order, received the Franciscan habit in Saint Boniface Church, Louisville, and took the name in religion of Sister Elizabeth. We celebrated these anniversaries quietly because of the War.

Last week, however, July 14, 1920, they celebrated for me. I, Sister Frances, the daughter of Hugh Walker, planter of Marion County, Kentucky, was the center of attraction. On the golden jubilee of my profession, I am the first and only Sister of our community who has spent a full half century as a professed nun.

The World War over, thank God, the Sisters felt as if they could celebrate again. Father Murray celebrated a high Mass for me in the college chapel, with the Sisters of the choir chanting. In the evening they prepared a special dinner. The students gave addresses. Mother Paul flattered me so that those at my table smiled at my blushes.

They asked me to respond. I had never given a public speech in my life. However, I did rise to my feet. But what I said I can scarcely remember. One thing I do recall. It had been in my mind all day.

"This is the happy golden jubilee of my profession," I said. "It was fifty-four and a half years ago that I first received the habit of Saint Francis--the twenty-first of January, 1866. It was in the parish church at Gethsemane from old Bishop Lavialle of Louisville.

"I thank you from the bottom of my heart for your kindnesses.

"Now please excuse me. I am very old, I am very excited and I am very happy and I want to go to my room."

****

Sister M. Frances Walker died on January 22nd, 1921, in her seventy-eighth year of life.

After her death, this was found in her handwriting:

"Here I sit at my desk in my little room at Mount Saint Clare. Now I can feel that I am growing slightly more tired each successive day. My room is in the old-fashioned tower of what was originally the Judge Chase mansion. A little stairway leads up to it. Until recently I climbed these stairs unaided. I am now too weak, ah, yes, too ill to leave my room...

"I am so glad that I have finished my story--not my story really, but the story of my dear community with whom I have suffered, with whom I have labored, and with whom, I trust, I have finally won the victory for the honor and glory of the dear Lord Christ.

"Yes, I must be getting very old because my mind goes back more and more to my old Kentucky days--to the tobacco fields of Marion County--to the distant roar of cannon at Perryville and the hectic period of the Civil War--to Pa and Ma Walker and the family.

"Mount Saint Clare is still Kentucky to me as long as my sweet friends of yore can comfort me in my decline--Mother Paul Carrico, Sister Carmel Schneider, Father Abbot Benedict at Mount Olivet and at Gethsemane. At night I so frequently dream of that saintliest Sister and friend that I ever knew, Jane de Chantal Batre. It will not be long now 'til I'm with her and Pa and Ma--and Christ, my Savior . . .

I Want to Go to My Room

****

At her death, Sister Frances' name appeared only briefly in the public news. It was a peculiar obituary, in a way, written by one of her friends. It told of her colorless life! "Sister Frances was remarkable for nothing," said the writer, "except for humble obedience."

What a curious remark regarding one who has given us such a story. Humility and obedience, yes. Colorless? No.

Select Time Line

1673	17th Century Dubuque, IA, area mentioned by Msgr. M. M. Hoffman, in *Antique Dubuque*
1790	Spalding, MD, Catholic family w/ Walker ancestors
1812	Fr. C. Nerincks started in log house
1848	Cistercians came to KY from France
1848	Gethsemane Trappists arrival
1849	Establishing Trappist monastery in Dubuque, IA
1853	Abbot Eutropius traveled KY, raising money
1855	School conducted since
1860	Willet conducted school until
1861	School on Charity Hill started
1862	Oct., Battle of Perryville, Capt. Warren killed
1864	Nov. 23, Caroline secretly takes habit from Fr. Dionysius at St. Boniface Church, Louisville, KY
1864?	Circa, (Dubuque) OSF started in Germany
1865	(Civil) War ends
1865	Bishop Spalding replaced by Bishop Lavialle
1865	Apr., Lizzie and Sally return to Charityville
1866	Jan. 21, Sally Walker and Lizzie Lillis given habits by Fr. Anselm at St. Boniface Church, Louisville, KY
1866	Mar. 14, agreement for beginning Order
1866	Spring, log school rising
1866	May 3, stations of cross erected, Feast of Finding of Cross
1868	Jun. 19, Feast of Sacred Heart, 5 sisters received
1868	Gas lights and furnace installed in new convent
1868	Jul. 17, Sr. Elizabeth replaced as superior by Sr. Mary Paula
1868	Abbot Benedict contract to protect Sr. Elizabeth
1868	Fall, Bishop Lavialle dies
1869	Feb. 23, lawyers meet at Caroline Warren's home to settle

1869	Apr. 18, we tentatively acquired a small addition of land
1869	Jul. 4, Mother (Mary) Paula tenders resignation
1869	Jul., farm willed to Corporation for United Schools
1869	Fat harvest at Olivet
1869	Dec. 16, letter to Abbot Benedict, hoping to stay
1870	(Dubuque) Franciscan Sisters in Franco-Prussian War
1870	Vatican Council
1870	Jul. 14, Sr. Jane de Chantal elected
1870	Nov., B. F. Mattingly visits
1870	Nov. 18, Abbot Benedict's sad visit to Mt. Olivet
1870	Dec., Dom Bruno Fitzpatrick letter
1871	Jan. 23, Hugh Walker writes statement regarding Sally's removal
1871	Sep. 7, letter Nannie Price, Antonia Willett
1871	Sep. 27, Hugh Walker letter of assurance
1872	Aug., meeting of General Chapter accepts Franciscans
1873	May, Mary Mooney, postulant
1873	Jul., election, Mother Jane de Chantal lacks vote
1873	Aug. 4, Mother Angela appointed
1873	Nov. 16, dreaded document by Mother Angela, move to Shelbyville, KY
1874	Jan., Mother Angela letter "no claim on (Olivet) land"
1874	Jun., fire of mysterious origin
1874-75	Mary Mooney (Sr. Agnes) and Julia Mattingly (Sr. Magdalen) enter
1875	(Dubuque) Franciscan Sisters, exiles, arrive in Iowa City
1875	Aug., bishop came to Shelbyville, KY, holy habits to seven
1875	Sr. Teresa (Ella McMahon) appointed mother superior
1877	Spring, Mother Teresa appealed to Franciscans at Oldenburg, IN
1877	Fall, benefactor Fr. Mertens moved from Shelbyville, KY
1877	Nov., wretched poverty, appeal for clothing
1877	Nov., Bishop McCloskey receives eight postulants
1877	Mother Teresa, discouraged, asks leave

Time Line

1878	Feb., Sr. Evangelista, then Dolorosa appointed temporarily
1878	Mar., Sr. Agnes (Mary Mooney) mother superior
1878-80	Chicago Hill teachers rebel
1878	Jul., Fr. Daly examined for lunacy, court
1878-90	Affair of Fr. Daly, Shelbyville, KY, Pastor
1879	Summer, Fr. Daly retires to home of friend
1880	Jul. 2, Mother Agnes appeals, "I sent last ten dollars."
1881	Nov., invitation to open St. Lawrence's school
1882	Nov., St. Jerome's school opened at Fancy Farm, KY
1883-85	Received some of "grandest" vocations--MD
1884	Fr. Godttbehoede offers, St. Patrick's, Minonk, IL
1884	Sep., Fr. Drury, now friend, invited Sr. Agnes
1884	Oct. 4, Feast of St. Francis, St. Clare's Academy
1884	Oct., Sisters commenced at St. Mary's, Whitesville, KY
1884	Oct. 21, Benefactor Ben F. Mattingly, $10,000
1884	Fall, Mother Agnes and Sr. Josephine begging in IN
1885	Jan. 20, Sr. Agnes' letter "besieged by our creditors"
1885	Aug. 3, death of Sr. Jane de Chantal
1887	Mar., Fr. Durbin's death
1887	Aug. 19, industrial school conveyed, Mt. Olivet
1887	Aug. 25, Sisters arrive at Gethsemane, bells ring
1887	Oct. 4, Feast of St. Francis--ignored
1889	Oct. 4, Bishop called first time in eight years
1889	Fall, epidemic of typhoid fever in Shelbyville, KY
1890	Apr., Bishop Hennessy receives Mother Agnes, Dubuque, IA
1890	Jul.-Oct., typhoid fever raged, Shelbyville, KY
1890	Aug., Abbot Benedict died, Abbot E. Chais-Bourbon succeeds
1890	Sep., first twelve sisters arrived Dubuque, IA
1890	Fall, Mother Agnes and community prepare to leave for IA
1890	Dec., snowy afternoon, 20 nuns, a girl and a dog arrive in Dubuque, IA
1890	Oct., Cecelia Anne and Agnes Mudd Dyer arrive
1891	Ill-fated Sisters of the Holy Ghost started in Dubuque, IA
1891	Jun., first Anamosa, IA, novice, Murcher, admitted

1891	Sep., Sr. Rose and four to St. Patrick's, Clinton, IA
1893	Spring, gave over whole "convent" for sanatorium
1893	Aug. 12, Clinton, IA, property purchased "Mt. St. Clare"
1893	Aug., Sr. Carmel announces "Move to Clinton!"
1893	Oct. 4, Feast of St. Francis, formal opening
1894	Summer, Sisters withdrawn from Anamosa, IA, school closed
1894	Sr. Michael's body moved for burial in Clinton, IA
1894	Fall, Fr. Powers asking for money owed and records
1895	Sep., new wing of building ready at Mt. St. Clare
1897	Complaints about Mother Agnes reach archbishop
1897	Aug., Mother Agnes illegally re-elected
1899	Apr., Corbin estate purchased for $6,000
1900	Jan. 1, novitiates demand investiture
1900	Jan. 27, election, Mother Agnes not candidate
1900	Jan. 27, Sr. Mary Magdalen elected superior
1903	Mother Magdalen re-elected
1903	Mt. Olivet School roofs leaked, cattle wandered in
1903	Mother Agnes runs for office and fails
1906	Jan. 27, election cancelled--investigation
1906	Jan. 30, Archbishop Keane investigates community
1906	Feb. 10, Sr. Paul elected by secret ballot
1906	Mother Agnes runs for office and fails
1907	Jul. 16, Fr. Powers, Anamosa, IA, writes joyful letter
1908	Aug., group of seventeen novices from Ireland
1909	Mother Paul re-elected, great expansion launched
1909	Aug., another five novices from Ireland
1910	May, another three novices from Ireland
1910	Nov. 13, 5-story Mt. St. Clare Academy cornerstone
1912	Mother Magdalen Mattingly elected
1914	Five novices arrive from Newfoundland
1915	Mother Paul elected mother general
1915	Eighteen novices from Newfoundland
1916	Another seventeen novices from Newfoundland
1918	Mother Paul re-elected mother general
1918	Carneys of Grinnell, IA, leave legacy, Grinnell Hospital bought
1920	Nine more novices from Newfoundland

Time Line

1920	Jul. 14, Golden Jubilee celebrated for Sr. Frances Walker
1920	Jul. 14, *Tribune* "The Jubilee of an Old Sister"
1921	Jan. 22, Sr. Frances Walker dies.
1944-48	Msgr M. M. Hoffman works on story. Typed copies.
1986	Sr. Augusta loans copy to Duane Hutchinson
1986-89	Hutchinson edits story, tells excerpts to Mt. St. Clare students and Sisters of St. Francis.
1990	First edition *Franciscans under Fire: Twenty Nuns a Girl and a Dog.*

Notes

FORWORD

1. (page xi) Monsignor Mathias Martin Hoffman also wrote *Antique Dubuque: 1673-1833, The Church Founders of the Northwest: Loras and Cretin and Other Captains of Christ* and *The Centennial History of the Archdioceses of Dubuque: 1837-1937.*

INTRODUCTION

2. (page xv) A postulant, she would later become Sister Louis.

3. (page xvii) Sister Augusta says that some of these were servants who came willingly with Sally Walker from her home.

CHAPTER 1.

4. (page 4) Francis of Assisi founded three orders: The first was the Friars Minor (gray friars), the second the Poor Clares and the third order the Brothers and Sisters of Penance (Tertiaries) founded about 1221 for lay people, monks and nuns. "Religious," usually an adjective, becomes a noun when used for the special Church vocations of the Third Order. A simple religious was distinct from a clerical nun.

5. (page 4) A Cistercian is a member of a monastic order founded at Citeaux, France, in 1098 under an austere Benedictine rule.

6. (page 4) Father Eutropius pamphlet, 1853. The pamphlet said, in part: "The desire of the Trappist monks would be likewise to procure the same benefits of instruction for the poor female children of the country, by establishing a school to be conducted by a lady of suitable age, and of unexceptionable piety, virtue and morals." And this promise of the school is signed by the Right Reverend Abbot Eutropius, and by Bishop Martin Spalding of

Louisville and also by the Comte de Charbonee, the French Bishop in Toronto, Canada, who gave a subscription.

7. (page 5) But he wasn't completely satisfied until Abbot Bruno of Ireland, who represented the General Chapter, visited the Gethsemane Abbey. He drew up an agreement with Bishop Spalding of Louisville which sanctioned free schools for boys and girls.

CHAPTER 2.

8. (page 10) Sisters of the Order of La Trappe of Mount Olivet named during property transaction.

It was a long document which contained the usual rules for maintaining a religious society. But two paragraphs in it were later to have considerable impact on our development.

I quote: "The undersigned ladies agree to have a dwelling house and school put up and provided with all necessary furniture at their own expense on the farm bought by the Rt. Rev. Abbot Benedict Berger residing at the Abbey of Gethsemane, known as Mount Olivet, said farm to remain the property of said ladies, or their associates who may join them thereafter for the same purpose, as soon as the money paid out by the Abbot Benedict Berger has been refunded either by the revenues of said farm or in any other way the Ladies think proper. And their object is to afford relief to as many persons of their sex as resources may allow; and to take charge of the female school promised by the Right Rev. Abbot Eutropius Proust, first Abbot of Gethsemane, and thus release forever said Abbey from that burden."

And the other paragraph read like this:

"The undersigned ladies who now undertake the work do declare to unite themselves and form under the name of Sisters of Our Lady of La Trappe of Mount Olivet, an establishment in which each of them will contribute personal labor and a certain sum determined by custom, or by the Superiors of the Order of La Trappe to whom they submit, whose rules and regulations they wish to embrace under the supervision of the Right Reverend Bishop of the Diocese of Louisville."

And the lengthy agreement was signed by all three of us as:

"Sister Mary Elizabeth--Mrs. Caroline Warren
"Sister Mary Margaret--Sally Walker
"Sister Mary Angela--Elizabeth Lillis."

Notes

CHAPTER 5.

9. (page 21) Two years later Pa wrote a declaration seeking to clarify this unfortunate affair:

"I, the undersigned, declare that my daughter, Sally Walker, went to Gethsemane in 1863 with her Aunt Caroline Warren, and she got into some difficulty and was sent home 1868 as sick; but I was soon told that it was only a pretext and that the true reason was that Father Jerome Moyen did not let her go to Communion for some months and that the Sisters could not keep her. Father Jerome asked me if I would sue the Abbot. I told him it was the last thing I would do to sue a priest or bishop. From what I could learn from my sister-in-law and Father Jerome and one other Reverend Father, their object was to get Father Benedict involved in a law-suit so as to impeach him before his superior. I was in secret consultation with them and was charged with secrecy by them. But when I found out that they were using my sister-in-law as a tool, I interfered and got the matter compromised.

"23rd January 1871
"Hugh Walker."

CHAPTER 7

10. (page 32) The full title in the Kentucky State Charter was "United Schools of the Abbey of Gethsemane for Girls at Mount Olivet."

CHAPTER 9.

11. (page 38) This letter, which was sent through councilors, Sisters Joseph and Angela, December 16, 1869, spoke with words which are still so vigorously illuminating of our sentiments, that I copy it in full:

"To Our Desolate Father M. Benedict, Abbot of Gethsemane:

"We, the undersigned Sisters of the Third Order of St. Francis, having made before the beginning of our Novitiate, a true and earnest promise to the Rt. Rev. M. Benedict, Abbot of Gethsemane, duly empowered by the Rt. Rev. P. G. Lavialle, Bishop of Louisville, to devote ourselves to the care and training of the girls of the female school, promised and established in favor of poor destitute girls, by the Abbey of Gethsemane, at Mount Olivet, having had an interview with his Lordship, Dr. McCloskey, Bishop of Louisville, and having heard many things about our removal, we do sincerely assure the Abbot, that if we leave him and his school, it will be against our will, and we declare to him that we are not satisfied that the Bishop objected to our making our perpetual vows, and allowed us to make vows only for one year, contrary to our Rule.

"Our Mistress of Novices having been called back to Indiana, the Bishop forbade us to appoint another Mistress, as our Statutes give the right to our Mother.

"We wish to accept the farm and the large new building offered to us as a payment to teach the school at Mount Olivet. We do not understand the opposition of the Bishop, who wrote in several of his letters that he would allow the Abbot to transfer us the farm at Mount Olivet, when the debts caused by the construction of the buildings would be paid. A good Catholic gentleman, Mr. Mattingly, paid all our debts, under the promise we made to say some prayers for him and his family. The Rt. Rev. Bishop saw our agreement before we received the money and gave our consent and now he is about to force us, to break up our agreement as well with our benefactor, as with the Abbot.

"Our Statutes, giving us the privilege not to be sent to another Community of our Order without our consent, we wish to die where we promised to stay and there to take care of our poor children as far as our means will allow us. We have no ambition, as likewise no desire to have a wealthy place and a large school; but we desire to remain poor and do good on a poor farm, forgotten and despised by the world."

CHAPTER 10

12. (page 44) Reference to the recent deeding of the properties to the United Schools of Gethsemane Abbey.

CHAPTER 11.

13. (page 52) Nostrums. *Merriam Webster's Seventh New Collegiate Dictionary* says a nostrum is "1. a medicine of secret composition recommended by its preparer but usually general repute. 2. A questionable remedy . . . "

CHAPTER 12.

14. (page 55) In the original agreement drawn up by Aunt Caroline, Sister Angela and Sister Margaret (Sally Walker, later Sister Frances) with Bishop Lavialle, one of the paragraphs had stated:
"The undersigned ladies who now undertake the work do declare to unite themselves under the name of Sisters of Our Lady of La Trappe of Mount Olivet, and submit to the Superior of the Order of La Trappe, whose rules and regulations they wish to embrace under the supervision of the Right Reverend Bishop of the Diocese of Louisville."

CHAPTER 13.

15. (page 60) Miss Mooney stayed but a few months at Mount Olivet. Since she was only twenty years of age, and her mother missed her and insisted on her return, she quietly gave in and went home. But she would re-enter later and eventually become the renowned Sister Agnes.

CHAPTER 15.

16. (page 68) As a novice, Elizabeth Batre (later Mother Jane de Chantal) had given as a "dowery," so to speak, several thousand dollars to help purchase the farm where the Sisters lived.
17. (page 68) Sister Jane de Chantal. Sister Jane de Chantal had loaned to J. Coleman of Louisville a sum at eight percent which was payable to the United Schools of Gethsemane.
18. (page 69) Ruth Price, Reason Price's daughter, had come into the order underage.

CHAPTER 16.

19. (page 74) Sister Bernard, Reason Price's daughter who pulled the rope the night of the fire, was involved in the "schism".

CHAPTER 17

20. (page 77) A forty-five minute train ride from Louisville.

21. (page 80) The famous plantation, featured in Stephen Foster's "My Old Kentucky Home," is across the road from part of Sister Augusta Carrico's family.

22. (page 80) Tantum ergo. An old Anglican hymnbook translates this:
> Therefore we, before him bending
> This great Sacrament revere;
> Types and shadows have their ending,
> For the newer rite is here;
> Faith, our outward sense befriending,
> Makes our inward vision clear.

CHAPTER 18

23. (page 83) See footnote number four on "religious."

24. (page 83) The full quotation: "Heaven knows, and I will freely admit, that these Franciscan ladies bequeathed to me by my predecessor are brave, zealous and pious, but I doubt if any bishop in Christendom has ever had the embroilments and contentious disorders of a sisterhood thrust upon him as I have had with them!"

CHAPTER 24

25. (page 111) Giving up the academy would be to give up one of our long-term dreams. Giving up music was almost unthinkable since we had two splendid teachers in Sister Carmel and Sister Magdalen Mattingly. But music was one of Abbot Benedict's phobias.

26. (page 111) "Dear Father," she said, "I feel the day is at hand when that God who brings peace to all men of good will is about to relieve my care worn mind by placing in our possession a home fixed permanently on unshaken ground and in that holy Name, Right Reverend Bishop, I beseech you on bended knees at your feet to grant me your blessing and consent to negotiate with Father Abbot."

27. (page 114) Sister Rose was our local superior at the time.

CHAPTER 25

28. (page 118) Editor's Note: It is interesting, however, that sixty-five years after the departure of the Sisters of St. Francis from Shelbyville, the pastor of Shelbyville wrote inviting the Franciscan Sisters to return. He said, "In all its nearly hundred years of existence the parish has never had a parochial school . . with the exception of the years that you good Sisters operated an academy . . . I make this appeal to you thinking that perhaps for sentimental reasons you may consider it. This site, I believe, is the cradle of your community in this country . . ."

The "cradle," of course, was Gethsemane Farm and Bishop Peter Lavialle of the Diocese of Louisville.

CHAPTER 27

29. (page 127) Her term "lazarette" referred to a kind of field hospital or aid station named after a church in Venice that maintained a hospital.

CHAPTER 29

30. (page 136) The property on which we established the original Mount St. Clare convent would later be known as Mount Alverno.

CHAPTER 31

31. (page 145) 30. The annals show: "The election of Rev. Mother Mary Magdalen Mattingly to be superior of the Community of the Third Order of St. Francis in Mount St. Clare, Clinton, Iowa, for the next three years.

"On the 27th day of January, 1900, in the Chapter room of Mount Alverno, Sister Mary Magdalen Mattingly was duly elected as Mother Superioress. Of all those having the right to vote, twenty Sisters were present, duly casting their ballots, Rev. J. A. Murray presiding by appointment of his Grace, the Most Rev. John Hennessy, D. D., Archbishop of Dubuque." [See page 155 of original copy of Monsignor Hoffman's manuscript.]

32. (page 146) Archbishop Diomede Falcoruo, the Papal Delegate in Washington, D. C. received a letter sent by

the friends of Mother Agnes accusing the Sisters of Mount St. Clare of breaches of discipline and other things. The exact contents of the letter were never made known to us.

Falcoruo notified Archbishop Hennessy's successor in Dubuque, John Joseph Keane. Archbishop Keane was a close friend of Cardinal Gibbons and Archbishop John Ireland.

Appendix

"The Jubilee of an Old Sister"
From the *Tribune*

Wednesday, July 14, 1920, the annals of the Sisters of St. Francis of the Immaculate Conception of Mount St. Clare, Clinton, Iowa, added to their numerous interesting events that of the first Golden Jubilee celebration of a member of the community.

Sister Mary Frances Walker of Marion County, Kentucky, was received into the community at its birth place, Mount Olivet, near Lebanon, Kentucky. She is the only living one of the intrepid band that faced the trials and difficulties attendant upon the foundation of a new community. She may, indeed, be said to be one of the foundation stones, since she was not such as to bring her into prominence before men, though we doubt not that in the annals kept in Heaven, her name holds place among the first.

Sister Mary Frances was born January 1, 1844, near Lebanon, Kentucky. Her father was Hugh Walker, a well-to-do farmer of that section, and, before the Civil War, a slave owner. Even up to the time of entering the convent in 1865, Sister Frances had been attended by her own servants, two of whom followed her, and did service on the convent farm for several years. To leave a home of luxury and ease to embrace poverty and hard work that she knew awaited her, was evidence of an extraordinary vocation and her life during the fifty-five years that have followed, has borne the fruits of its early promise. Inclined to piety from her earliest years, her only ambition was for a life of prayer.

The Solemn High Mass of celebration took place at Mount St. Clare at 7:30 A.M. The Rev. Father Murray was the preacher of the occasion and spoke in glowing words of the life that had been spent in such sacred consecration until it had reached its golden milestone--of the glory of the perseverance that soon must receive its eternal reward.

At 6:30 P.M. the program appropriate to the occasion was given by members of the community.

(Sister Frances, commenting about this said, "I liked the article for two special reasons: first it spoke of Pa, the Kentucky tobacco farmer; and then although it referred to the celebration as a Golden Jubilee it gave the correct number of years that I had spent as a bride of Christ--fifty-five.)

Index of Names

A

Agnes
  Mother xii, xv, 82, 83, 85, 87, 88, 89, 92, 93, 95, 96, 100, 101, 103, 105, 107, 108, 109, 110, 111, 113, 114, 115, 116, 118, 121, 125, 126, 127, 128, 129, 132, 133, 134, 137, 139, 140, 142, 143, 145, 146, 149, 150, 153, 154, 176
  Sister (see Mary Mooney) 15, 74, 82, 94, 100, 147, 173
Alabama
  Mobile 33
Albrecht
  Dom Edmond 122
Aloysius
  Sister 15, 97
Alverno
  Mount (see Mount Saint Clare) xi, 141, 145, 157, 175
Amata
  Sister 27, 28, 31, 37, 38
Anamosa
  Academy 132
Angela
  Mother (see Lizzie Lillis) 61, 63, 64, 65, 67, 68, 69, 70, 71, 74, 75, 77, 78, 90, 95
  Sister (see Lizzie Lillis), 10, 12, 16, 32, 34, 38, 41, 44, 52, 56, 59, 60, 71, 171, 173
Angelica
  Sister (see Cynthia Murcher) 82, 139, 145, 149
Ann
  Saint
    Academy 157
Anselm
  Father 9, 12
  Sister 15
Anthony
  Saint
    School 157
Antique Dubuque
  1673-1833 169
Antonelli
  Cardinal 43
Antonia
  Mother 15, 16, 27, 31, 37
  Sister 80
Antony
  Sister 15
Arms and the Monk! The Trappist Saga in Mid-America xi
Assissium
  Sister 118
Augusta
  Empress 127
  Sister (see Sister Augusta Carrico) xi, xii, xix
Autro-Prussian War 127

B

Bach
  Johann Sebastian 106
Bacon
  Joseph
    Dr. 146
Badin
  Father xvi
Baltimore
  Lord 99
Baptist
  John 21
Baptists 111
Batre
  Charles 33, 34
  de Chantal
    Jane 160
      Sister 56
    Elizabeth (see Jane de Chantal) 69, 110, 173
    Mrs. Charles (see Jane de Chantal), 33
Beatrice
  Sister 74
Beauregard
  Pierre
    General 33
Beavan

Mary Jane (see Sister
    Paula, Mary Jane
    Beavan), 15, 16
Belgium 59
Benedict
  Abbot (see Abbot
    Benedict Berger) 35,
    43, 45, 46, 48, 49, 50,
    60, 63, 64, 68, 74, 78,
    102, 109, 111, 112, 114,
    121, 122, 134
  Father 44, 48, 58, 62, 70,
    73, 75, 91, 95, 100, 107,
    160, 171
  Saint 55
  Sister 52, 64, 65, 67, 69, 70,
    72, 73
Benoit
  Father 107
Benz
  Brothers 94
Berger
  Benedict
    Abbot (see Abbot
      Benedict)4, 9, 11,
      12, 15, 16, 19, 21, 26,
      31, 170
    Father 5, 20, 171
Bernard
  Sister (see Ruth Price) 61,
    67, 69, 70, 74, 82, 83,
    84, 85
Bismarck
  Chancellor 127
Bleavan
  Mary Jane 20
Bonacum
  Bishop 118
Bonaventure
  Father 44, 50
  Sister (see Elizabeth
    Jarboe) 15, 25, 26, 28
Boniface
  Saint
    Church 8, 9, 44, 159
Boone
  Daniel xvi
Booth
  John Wilkes 132
Bourton
  Edward Chaix
    Father 60
Brag
  General 3
Bridget
  Saint
    school 74
Bruno
  Abbot 170
Buckingham
  Eliza 52

C

Cahill
  Mary 5
Calhoun
  Major 73
Calvary Hill 5, 8, 19, 22, 47,
  50, 61, 112
Cambron 8, 20
  Caroline (see Caroline
    Cambron Warren and
    Sister Elizabeth)
  Henry 21
  Isabelle 131
Canada
  Toronto 170
Carmel
  Sister (see Rose
    Schneider) 106, 132,
    135, 136, 174
Carney 158
Caroline
  Aunt 9, 90
  Sister (see Sister Caroline
    Gehringer)
Carolon
  Father 133
Carrico 106, 158, 159
  Augusta
    Sister (see Sister
      Augusta) xi, 169,
      174
  Edna 159
  Laura (see Mother Paul of
    the Cross), 106, 149,
  Marie 159
  Minnie 159
  Mother Paul of the Cross
    xii, 159, 160
  Nola 159

Index of Names

Rena 159
Catholic University of
   America 146, 158
Cecil
   Constantine 21
Cecilia
   Saint
      School 74
   Sister 80
*Centennial History of the
   Archdioceses of Dubuque
   1837-1937* 169
Chaix-Bourbon
   Edward
      Abbot (see Abbot
         Edward) 121
      Father 19
Chambige
   Father 91
Charity
   Sisters of xvi, 4, 8, 80, 91,
      111
Charity Hill 7, 8
Charityville (see Charity
   Hill), 8, 22, 61
Chase
   Judge 136, 160
Cheshire 64
Chicago Hill 74, 78, 81, 83,
   84, 93, 94, 95, 96, 97, 107,
   110, 113, 125
*Church Founders of the
   Northwest: Loras and
   Cretin and Other
   Captains of Christ* 169
Cimeoni
   Cardinal 84
Cistercians 4, 44, 122, 169
   France 41, 45
Citeaux 55
   Order of 56
Civil War xvi, xviii
Clare
   Saint
      Feast of 136
      Mount 136, 139, 141,
         145, 146, 147,
         149, 158, 160,
         175, 177
      Academy 74, 157,
         158

Sisters of 81
College xii, 106
Durham Hall xi
Junior College 158
Clares
   Poor 169
Cleary
   Regis
      Mother xi
Clemanceau
   George 122
Clement
   Father 140
   L. P. 71
Coghland
   J. I.
      Father 117, 118
Coleman
   J. 173
Colorado 155
   Denver 80
   Rockies 99
Columba
   Mary
      Sister (see Victoria
         Curtsinger) 106
Connecticut
   New Haven 52
Corbin 141
Crane
   Father 117
Crury
   Edward
      Father 71
Curtsinger
   Victoria (see Sister Mary
      Columba) 106

D

Daly
   Hugh
      Father 81, 87, 88, 89,
         90, 91, 94, 115, 116,
         117
Davis
   Bishop 158
de Chantal
   Jane 173

Mother 44, 45, 46, 48,
49, 50, 51, 52, 55, 58,
59, 60, 63, 141
Sister (see Mrs.
Charles Batre), 33,
34, 38, 39, 40, 44, 65,
68, 69, 73, 78, 79, 82,
83, 88, 90, 95, 96,
102, 107, 108, 110,
122, 173
de Hodiamont
Constant
Baron 59, 73
Devied
Father 91
Dionysius
Father 8
District of Columbia
Washington 176
dog
Saint Bernard
Carlos xv, 116, 126
Dolorosa
Sister 77, 81, 85, 100, 102,
113, 115, 125, 133, 142
Dominica
Sister 50, 52, 63, 67, 73, 74,
82, 85
Drury
Edmund
Father 78, 83, 84, 94,
95, 97, 107, 117
Dubuque 128
Center for History xiii
Durbin
Eliseus
Father 92
Dyer
Agnes Mudd 132
Cecelia Anne 132
Miss 131

E

Edward
Abbot (see Abbot
Edward Chaix-
Bourbon) 121
Prior 69
Elizabeth
Sister (see Caroline
Cambron and Caroline
Cambron Warren), 10,
12, 13, 16, 19, 20, 26,
159
England
Trappestine convents 58
Ephraim
Prior 48
Etienne
Father 58
Eutropius
Abbot (see Eutropius
Proust) 5, 43
Father 4, 169
Evangelista
Sister 77, 81, 82

F

Falcoruo
Diomede
Archbishop 176
Finn
Mary 15
Fitzpatrick
Dom Bruno
Abbot 44, 45, 46, 47, 48,
49, 52, 55, 56, 57,
117
Flint
Island 34, 38, 39
Foster
Stephen 79, 174
France xvi, 10, 44
Alsace-Lorraine 127
Mortgane 57
Frances
Sister (see Sally Walker
and Sister Margaret)
xi, xii, xviii, xix, 31, 52,
60, 64, 67, 70, 83, 87,
88, 114, 118, 131, 135,
141, 145, 159, 161, 173,
178
Francis
Saint 39, 75, 95, 102, 118,
160
Church xi
Hospital 157
Industrial School 125

of Assisi xv, 169
Sisters of the
Immaculate
Conception xi
Third Order of 4, 8, 9,
10, 12, 20, 57, 83,
175
Sisters of xvii, 9, 12,
32, 37, 60, 71, 90,
157, 171, 175
Franciscan Sisters
German 15
Franco-German War 127
Friars Minor
gray friars 169

G

Gabriel
Sister 15
Gambou
Father 111
Gawley
Dr. 133, 136
Gehringer
Caroline
Sister xi
German State Bank 67
Germany xvi, 125, 159
Hereford 127
Gethsemane (see
Gethsemane,
Kentucky) 63
Abbey of 4, 15, 16, 26, 49,
107, 114, 121, 127, 170,
172
Abbot of 63, 171
College 121
Farm 4, 175
United Schools of 28, 40,
64, 68, 69, 171, 172, 173
Gibbons
Cardinal 176
Gibson
Mike xiii
Gillim
Florence 126
Godttbehoede
Lucan
Father 99
Graham

Estella 15
Green
John 132
Grinnell
Hospital 158

H

Hancock
Miss 105
Harmon
Silas xii
Harris
Captain 113
Harwood
C. M. 89
Hennessy
John
Archbishop 118, 119,
125, 128, 133, 134,
135, 139, 142, 145,
175
Higdon
Allie (see Sister Mary
Lawrence) 106
Hill
Mr. 21
Hoffman
Mathias Martin 169
Monsignor xi, xii, xviii,
xix, 169, 175
Hogan
Sheriff 154
Holy Ghost
Sisters of the 133
Hutchinson
Duane xiii

I

Ignatius
Sister 15
Illinois 134
Central Station xv, 126
Chicago xv, 101, 121, 149,
150
Heights 149, 150, 154
Kickapoo 139
Macomb 145, 157
Minonk 100

Toluca 145, 157
Immaculate Conception
    School 157
Indiana 37, 134, 172
    Franciscans 27
    Lexington xii
    Oldenburgh 15, 17, 19, 26,
        31, 37, 41, 78, 103
        convent 16
    Vincennes 15
Iowa xii, xvi, 48, 60, 81, 87, 97,
        100, 101, 118
    Akron 157
    Anamosa 126, 127, 128,
        132, 133, 135, 136,
        137, 139, 153
    Arts Council xi
    Cedar Rapids 133, 136
    Clinton xi, xvii, 106, 132,
        135, 136, 139, 145,
        146, 153, 157, 158,
        175, 177
        Saint Patrick's School
            135
    Cresco 157
    Dubuque xv, xvii, 44, 118,
        119, 125, 126, 127,
        131, 133, 139, 142,
        147, 150
        Archibishop of 175
    Dyersville xi
    Epworth 157
    Grinnell 158
    Hawarden 145, 157
    Iowa City 128
    Keystone 135
    Mason City 125, 133, 157
    Petersville 131, 157
    Sioux City 126
    State Reformatory 128
    Stone City 132
    Tama 157
    Vail 125, 157
Ireland xvi, 159, 170
    County Waterford
        Cappoquin 56
    John
        Archbishop 176
    Melleray
        Mount
            Abbey 45, 56

Italy
    Venice 175

J

Jackson
    Andrew 28
Jarboe
    Elizabeth (see Sister
        Bonaventure) 15
Jerome
    Saint
        School 99
    Father (see Father
        Jerome Moyen)
Joachim
    Saint
        Academy 157
Johannes
    Father 127
John
    Saint
        School 157
Johnson
    William
        Governor 110
        Lieutenant 69
        Senator 28, 34
Joseph
    Saint 110
        High School 157
    Sister 15, 32, 34, 38, 39, 41,
        59, 74, 87, 88, 171
Josephine
    Sister 103
Josephite
    Fathers 107

K

Keane
    John Joseph
        Archbishop 146, 147,
            149, 150, 176
Kentucky xii, xv, 4, 22, 127,
    139
    Bardstown xvi, 43, 60, 65,
        67, 70
    Berea xii
    Calvary xvi

Index of Names

Chicago (see Chicago Hill), 94, 96
Danville 31
Fancy Farm 99, 106, 116, 126, 139, 149, 159
Franciscans 55
Franklin 31
Gethsemane xvi, xvii, 9, 25, 35, 41, 43, 45, 56, 57, 58, 60, 67, 73, 102, 109, 112, 117, 127, 160, 171
    Trappists 43
Henderson 34
Herdinsburg 113
Holy Cross xvi
Knottsville 99, 111, 115, 159
Lebanon xvi, 177
Lexington xii
Lieutenant-governor of 34
London 108
Loretto xvi
    Academy 12
Louisville xi, xii, xvii, 8, 21, 26, 28, 41, 43, 44, 58, 60, 67, 71, 74, 75, 80, 88, 89, 91, 94, 95, 99, 106, 109, 111, 113, 115, 125, 159, 160, 170, 173, 174, 175
    Bishop of the Diocese 10, 172
    Courier-Journal 89
    Diocese of 9, 173
    Franciscan Monastery 103
    Saint Boniface Church 9
    Saint Louis cemetery 92, 125
Marion County 7, 8, 20, 31, 32, 51, 65, 74, 99, 101, 139, 159, 160, 177
    Cartwright's Creek 21
    Saint Charles 113
Maysville 158
Mead County 27
Nazareth xvi, 3, 80
    Academy 12

Nelson County 51
    Mount Olivet 32, 109
Owensboro 99, 106
Perryville 160
    Battle of 3, 65
Saint Charles xvi
Saint Rose xvi
Shelbyville 63, 64, 65, 67, 68, 72, 73, 74, 75, 77, 79, 81, 85, 87, 89, 90, 91, 93, 95, 99, 100, 109, 111, 112, 114, 115, 116, 117, 118, 125, 133, 139, 143, 151, 175
Union County 15
Washington County 71
Whitesville 99, 115, 139
King
    Father 99
Kister
    John 16
Ku Klux Klan 69

L

La Trappe 34, 47
    Abbots of 57
    Angelic Nuns of 56
    Order of 170, 173
    Sisters of the 10, 55, 170, 173
Lantz
    F. J.
        Father 145
Lavialle
    Peter Joseph
        Bishop 9, 10, 11, 12, 15, 21, 39, 55, 109, 160, 171, 173, 175
Lawrence
    Mary (see Allie Higdon)
        Sister 106
    Saint
        School 99
Lillis
    Elizabeth "Lizzie" (see Sister Angela) 3, 4, 6, 8, 9, 10, 61, 75, 171
Lincoln
    Abraham 132
Loras College

186 FRANCISCANS UNDER FIRE

Center for Dubuque
History xiii
Loretto
  Sisterhood Friends of
    Mary at the Foot of the
    Cross 113
  Sisters of xvi, 4, 8, 27, 95
Louis
  Sister 169
Louisiana
  New Orleans 33, 110
Lourdes
  Grotto of 107
Loyola University 158
Luckett
  Francel 44
Luther
  Martin 59

M

Mader
  Amalia 159
Magdalen
  Mary
    Mother 74, 145, 146
    Sister (see Sister
      Magdalen Mattingly
      and Julia Mattingly)
      81, 113, 116, 127, 141,
      142, 149
Margaret
  Sister (see Sally Walker
    and Sister Frances)
    10, 31, 170, 173
Mary
  Saint
    of the Angels 87
    School 99, 157
Maryland
  Baltimore xvii, 15, 43, 132
    Archbishop of 9
    Catholics 8, 99
    Charles County 21
Mattingly
  Ben F. xii, 22, 23, 31, 35,
    38, 45, 46, 47, 50, 51,
    59, 74, 109, 172
  Julia (see Mother Mary
    Magdalen) 74
  Louis Edward xii

Magdalen
  Mother xii
  Sister 95, 97, 145, 174,
    175
McCloskey 89
  William
    Bishop 21, 25, 26, 27,
      28, 31, 35, 37, 38,
      172, 41, 43, 48, 50,
      52, 57, 60, 62, 63, 64,
      67, 69, 72, 75, 77, 80,
      81, 83, 84, 88, 89, 90,
      91, 93, 94, 97, 100,
      101, 108, 111, 114,
      115, 116, 118, 121,
      134
McDonald
  Miss 15
McGlone 15
McLaughlin
  E. J.
    Dean 136, 140, 146
McMahon 80
  Ella (see Sister Teresa),
    77
McNicholas
  Father 38, 39
Melleray
  Mount
    Abbey 45
Mercy
  Sisters of 126, 133, 136, 75
Mertens
  Father 77, 78
Michael
  Sister 115, 121, 136
Miles
  Edward 21
Mill Hill
  College 107
Mississippi 33
  River xv, 48, 99, 154
  Vicksburg 22
Missouri 157
  Doniphon 159
  Saint Louis 59, 75
    Sisters of Mercy
      126, 133, 136
    University 117
Mooney

Index of Names

Mary (see Sister Agnes)
60, 74, 173
Agnes
   Sister 81
Morrison
   Mrs. 113
Moyen
   Jerome
      Father 20, 21, 23, 25, 171
Mudd
   Samuel A.
      Dr. 132
   Mary Clare 132
Muldoon
   Bishop P. J. 158
Murcher
   Cynthia (see Sister Angelica) 139
Murray
   J. A.
      Father 135, 136, 145, 146, 158, 159, 175, 177
My Old Kentucky Home 174

N

Nebraska 157
   Lincoln 118
   Omaha 126
   Wesleyan University xii
Nerincks
   Charles
      Father xvi, 4, 113
New Haven
   Sisters School of 110
New Mexico 155
New York 76, 105
   Graymoor 155
Newfoundland 15, 159
Newman
   J. E.
      Judge 21, 23, 28, 34, 70
North Carolina 33
Nova Scotia
   Trappist Abbey 64

O

O'Dowd
   Peter
      Father 131
O'Grady
   Joseph
      Father 112
Ohio
   Cincinnati xvii, 15, 45, 75, 77, 84, 89, 101, 116
   Archbishop Elder of 84
   River 99
Oldham
   Mrs. 12
Olivet
   Mount xvii, 12, 15, 16, 17, 20, 21, 22, 25, 26, 31, 32, 33, 34, 35, 37, 38, 39, 40, 43, 44, 45, 48, 49, 50, 52, 55, 57, 58, 59, 60, 61, 63, 64, 65, 67, 68, 69, 70, 71, 72, 73, 74, 75, 77, 83, 94, 102, 107, 109, 110, 111, 114, 115, 121, 122, 125, 143, 151, 158, 160, 170, 172, 173, 177
   Convent 16
   Primary School for Girls 11, 12, 112
   Sisters of 20, 21, 22
   United Schools of the Abbey of Gethsemane for Girls at 28, 40, 64, 68, 69, 171, 172
Olivia
   Mother 103
Orsisi
   Brother 16
Our Lady of the Angels 79, 81, 93, 95, 114, 116

P

Palais
   de Saint
      Bishop 15

Paschal
    Sister 145
Patrick
    Saint
        School 99, 135, 157
Paul
    of the Cross
        Mother (see Laura
            Carrico) 106, 149,
            150, 153, 154, 158,
            159
        Sister 149
    Saint
        School 157
Paula
    Mother 27, 31, 32, 34, 35,
        37, 38, 39, 41, 44
    Sister 15, 19, 40
Pechan
    Archbishop 101
Pellier
    Father 34
Penance
    Brothers and Sisters of
        169
Pendleton
    Andrew Jackson 70, 73,
        101
    Patience 20, 28, 70, 73,
        101
Pennsylvania
    Gettysburg 22
Phillipa
    Sister 38
Piercall 106
Poor
    Sisters of the 85
Powers
    Robert
        Father 127, 128, 132,
            136, 137, 138, 140,
            153, 154
Price
    Nannie 51
    Reason 51, 74, 173
    Ruth (see Sister Bernard)
        44, 51, 173
Proust
    Eutropius
        Abbot (see Abbot
            Eutropius) 170

Purcall
    Archbishop 43

Q

Quigley
    Archbishop 150, 151, 154
Quinlan
    John
        Bishop 33

R

Rapier
    Sylvester 71
Reed
    J. F. 91
Regis
    Mother xi
Roberta
    Sister 127
Roberts 106
Rock
    Father 99
Rose
    Sister 114, 115, 135, 174
Russell
    Dr. 44
    Father 45
Ryan
    Lula (see Sister Mary
        Xavier) 106
    Nora 159
    Roger
        Father 118, 126, 142
    Xavier
        Sister 133

S

Schneider
    Carmel
        Sister 160
    Frederick 106
    Rose (see Sister Mary
        Carmel) 106
Sexton
    John 45
    Miss 15
Shea

Index of Names

Con xvi, 126
Simon
  Father 60, 63
Smith
  Frank 16
  Mary
    Sister xii
Spalding
  Martin J.
    Archbishop xvii, 43
    Bishop 9, 39, 170

T

Tennessee
  Knoxville 34
  Lebanon 21
  Marion County 3
  Nashville 3, 20, 23, 34
  Shiloh
    Battle of 34
Teresa
  Mother 77, 78, 79, 80, 90
  Sister (see Ella
    McMahon) 77, 149
Tertians 9, 10
The Story of Loras College xi
Trappist
  abbey xvi
  brothers 49
  Order 5
Trappistines 26
Trappists 4, 10, 34, 43
  French 122
Turkey
  Constantinople 76
Twenty Nuns, a Girl and a Dog xiii

U

Ubaldus
  Father 103
Ursulines 126

V

Van Borah
  Catherine 59
Van Wie

Miss 105
Veronica
  Sister 80
Vincent
  Sister 67, 82
Viola
  Father 63, 71, 95
Vittitow
  Sam 16
Vowels
  Richard 40

W

Walker 31
  homestead 8
  Hugh xviii, 16, 53, 54, 70, 113, 159, 171, 177
  Kentucky ancestors 43
  Sally xi, (see Sister Frances and Sister Margaret), xii, xviii, 3, 5, 6, 7, 25, 28, 169, 170, 171, 173
  Frances
    Sister xviii, 56, 160, 177
Walsh
  Father 50
War of the States 9
Ward
  Father 117
Warren
  Baptist 3
  Captain 3
  Caroline Cambron xii, 3, 4, 5, 6, 7, 8, 9, 10, 11, 12, 13, 21, 25, 34, 127, 159, 170, 173
Waters
  Julia 10, 12, 15
Willett 106
  Antonia 51
  Louisa 5

X

Xavier
  Mother (see Lula Ryan) 127

Sister 106, 142

Y

Young and Fair Is Iowa xi

Z